CULTURES OF THE WORLD

ARGENTINA

Ethel Caro Gofen

MARSHALL CAVENDISH
New York • London • Sydney

Reference edition published 1998 by
Marshall Cavendish Corporation
99 White Plains Road
Tarrytown
New York 10591

© Times Editions Pte Ltd 1994, 1991

Originated and designed by
Times Books International, an imprint of
Times Editions Pte Ltd

Printed in Singapore

Library of Congress Cataloging-in-Publication Data:
Gofen, Ethel, 1937–
    Argentina/ Ethel Gofen.
        p. cm.—(Cultures of the World)
    Includes bibliographical references.
    Summary: Profiles the history, geography,
    government, and people of Argentina and
    highlights the country's main cultural and social
    traditions.
    ISBN 1-85435-381-0
    1. Argentina. [1. Argentina.] I. Title. II. Series.
F2808.2.G64   1991
982—dc20   90–23159
                    CIP
                    AC

INTRODUCTION

The Argentina of the romantic imagination is a land of spectacular scenery, colorful gauchos, dramatic tango dancers, polo players, and soccer champions. The real Argentina has all these, plus a sophisticated culture centered in Buenos Aires and a stormy history dominated by charismatic and often controversial leaders.

The name Argentina means "silver," and this fertile country has long fostered explorers' dreams of unlimited wealth. The political strife and harsh economic realities of the past 50 years have deferred those dreams. What remains is the exceptional beauty of the country, the pride of its highly educated citizens, and their enduring wish to attain for their country a respected position in world affairs.

CONTENTS

Argentina is blessed with a beautiful countryside, friendly people and a colorful culture.

CONTENTS

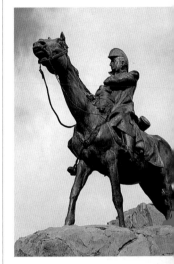

Argentina: land of heroes
and legends from an
exciting and glorious
past.

GEOGRAPHY

WHETHER YOU DREAM of mountain peaks, sandy beaches, or fertile plains, the vast South American country of Argentina has them all. Its terrain stretches from the subtropical north to sub-Antarctic regions of the south. One major reason that its climate and geography are so dramatically diverse is that the country is so long—about 2,300 miles. Since it lies in the Southern Hemisphere, the climate is usually hottest in the north, nearer the Equator, and coldest in the south.

Argentina is the eighth largest country in the world. In South America, only Brazil is larger in area and population. The land mass of Argentina covers almost 1.1 million square miles and measures 868 miles across at its broadest point.

Argentina's neighbors are Bolivia and Paraguay to the north, Brazil and Uruguay to the east, and Chile to the south and west. The Atlantic Ocean on the east and south and the snow-capped Andes Mountains to the west form long natural borders.

Argentineans are proud of their country's great natural beauty. And, as a country with long stretches of mountains and seashore, Argentina boasts some famous extremes of elevation. The Salinas Grandes, or Great Salt Mines, is the lowest place on the South American continent—131 feet below sea level. Near the Chilean border, the summit of Mt. Aconcagua, an extinct volcano, is the highest place in the Western Hemisphere (22,831 feet).

Opposite: **The Perito Moreno Glacier in Patagonia. Glaciers are actually very large blocks of ice.**

Below: **The desert of northwest Argentina. Argentina's climate varies more than that of most of the world's countries.**

NORTHERN ARGENTINA

The northern part of Argentina is heavily forested, low, wet, and hot. Early settlers called one area of the north the Gran Chaco, or hunting ground, to distinguish it from the pampas, a vast cattle grazing region farther south.

` Few people live in the forests of the Chaco. The region is rich in forest products, but its fertility is limited in some parts by swamps and in other places by periodic dry spells. Winters in the Chaco are dry, while summers are humid, with temperatures rising as high as 120°F. Yearly rainfall ranges from 60 inches in the northeast to 20 inches in the west.

Another part of the north is called Mesopotamia, which includes the province of Entre Ríos and Misiones. Both names mean "between rivers." These lowlands lie between the Paraná and Uruguay rivers. Rolling grassy plains, rivers, and swamps are their chief features. The climate is warm and wet all year round. Ranchers raise cattle, horses, and sheep here. Farmers grow flax, wheat, and fruits.

The Misiones province in northeastern Mesopotamia has heavy rains, thick forests, and many waterfalls. The most spectacular is the dramatic Iguazú Falls on the Brazilian border. The region's most famous crop is the holly plant, used to make *yerba mate* ("ZHER-bah MAH-teh"). This brewed herbal tea, the gaucho's favorite drink, is served all over Argentina.

Palm savannahs on the wet and swampy lowlands of the Entre Ríos.

IGUAZÚ FALLS: A WORLD-CLASS TOURIST DESTINATION

Misiones, in northeastern Mesopotamia, has heavy rains, thick forests, and many waterfalls. The most spectacular scenic location is the dramatic Iguazú Falls on the Brazilian border. Imagine the thrill of being the first Spanish explorer to discover this gorgeous cascade in 1541.

Iguazú is a Guaraní Indian word meaning Great Water. More than 275 waterfalls stretch around an 8,100-foot-wide arc of the Río Iguazú. They fall roughly 270 feet and splash over a series of islands, creating spectacular sprays and rainbows. The largest waterfall, called the Devil's Throat, is more than 350 feet high.

The falls are set in a national park with 132,500 acres of tropical jungle. A wildlife reserve shelters hundreds of species of birds, reptiles, fish, 25 species of butterflies, orchids, monkeys, parrots, and pumas. Nature lovers also appreciate the hundreds of different species of trees and tropical plants.

A Hollywood movie, *The Mission*, set at Iguazú Falls, showed vivid scenes of the life of native Indians, Jesuit priests, and Spanish colonists 250 years ago. It won the 1986 Cannes Film Festival award for best picture and also won an Oscar for best cinematography.

THE PAMPAS

More than two-thirds of Argentina's people live in the pampas. Most cities, industries, and important transportation facilities are also in this part of the country. The capital, Buenos Aires, and several other large cities are located there. Argentina's wealth comes mainly from this region.

The pampas are flat, fertile, temperate plains in the central part of the country. They stretch from the Atlantic Ocean to the Andes, covering one-fifth of Argentina.

The word "pampas" comes from a Guaraní Indian word meaning "level land." Visitors are astounded when they see these plains stretching endlessly to the horizon in all directions, with barely a tree or stone to catch the eye, and looking as flat as the sea. While there is plenty of rain in the eastern part, about 40 inches per year, the climate becomes drier to the west. Much of the country's chief crops—wheat, corn, and alfalfa—are raised in its rich soil. Vast herds of cattle graze on the drier western plains. Farmers also raise flax and hogs here.

THE ANDES

The western part of Argentina, bordering on Chile, is marked by the huge mountain range of the Andes. Not many people live in this rugged area. A small group of Indians raise sheep in the northern part of the Argentinean Andes. Miners dig for iron ore, uranium, and other metals. Although the earliest Spanish settlements were in the Andes, these days only about 15% of the people live there.

Just east of the Andes is a region called the Piedmont. In these low mountains and desert valleys, farmers grow important crops, especially sugarcane, corn, cotton, and fruit, all for export.

Mt. Aconcagua is the highest mountain in South America.

Most Argentinean wines come from the vineyards near Mendoza and the grapes of San Juan in the Piedmont. The dry climate, sandy soil, and year-round sunshine are ideal for the wine industry.

West of Mendoza lies Mt. Aconcagua, meaning "Stone Guard" in an Indian dialect. At 22,831 feet, it is the highest peak in the Western Hemisphere. Near here is the Uspallata Pass, the Camino de los Andes. This pass leads into Chile at a height of 12,600 feet.

11

THE SOUTHERNMOST TOWN IN THE WORLD

The southernmost town in the world, Ushuaia (an Indian word pronounced "oo-shoo-AH-yah"), is situated in Argentina. Its weather is almost always chilly, and the nearby mountains are usually snow-capped. The 20,000 people of Ushuaia can look south across the

waters of the Beagle Channel toward the South Pole, some 650 miles away.

People in Ushuaia have only about seven hours of daylight in the winter. In the summer, they enjoy daylight for about 17 hours each day.

PATAGONIA

Patagonia covers more than a quarter of Argentina and includes windswept dry plateaus crossed by many deep canyons. It lies in the rain shadow of the Andes, resulting in stretches of cool desert.

In the west are beautiful resort areas of lakes and mountains, while in the far south it is always cool and often foggy, with many storms. Although there is no real summer, ocean currents keep winter temperatures

Except where the government has built irrigation canals, most of Patagonia has such poor soil and little rainfall that it cannot support crops.

moderate. At the southern tip of South America is the island of Tierra del Fuego, or Land of Fire. It was named after the Ona and Yagana Indian campfires seen by early European sailors. Soon, European settlers and Chileans arrived to raise sheep on large ranches and grow vegetables and fruit on irrigated farms. Only about 1% to 3% of Argentina's population live in Patagonia. It provided a perfect hideout for the legendary bank robbers of North America—Butch Cassidy and the Sundance Kid.

ARGENTINA'S WATERS

More than 1,600 miles of the length of Argentina are bounded by the Atlantic Ocean. Several large bays dot the seacoast. The most important is formed by the Río de la Plata (River Plate), the longest river in Argentina, which flows between Argentina and Uruguay.

The Paraná River system drains northern and much of central Argentina. The giant rivers in Argentina serve as boundaries and as important transportation arteries.

The drainage patterns of Argentina's rivers and lakes are greatly affected by the height of the Andean mountains. In the south, a series of Argentinean lakes empty into the Pacific Ocean through Chile. But after heavy rains, they send their extra water into the Atlantic Ocean. This happens because the lakes sit almost directly on top of the continental divide, a line that separates waters flowing east from those flowing west.

A lake noted for its special beauty is Nahuel Huapí. It extends for 200 square miles at 2,500 feet above sea level at the heart of a nature reserve and resort area in the southern Andes. A natural feature of great interest to visitors is the Perito Moreno Glacier in Patagonia. The glacier moves five yards a day, noisily shattering icebergs in its path and raising a dramatic explosion of spray.

The llama is commonly found in the highlands of the northern Andean plateau.

COLORFUL WILDLIFE

Some of the unusual animals that live in Argentina include the armadillo, opossum, coatimundi, tapir, jaguar, howler monkey, giant anteater, and puma or mountain lion.

The guanaco is a small relation of the camel that, unlike its larger cousin, has no hump. It is the common ancestor of the llama, alpaca and vicuña. These animals roam the northern Andean plateau. The alpaca and vicuña contribute hides and wool to the economy.

The Patagonian cavy is related to the guinea pig. The vizcacha, a burrowing animal of the pampas, digs far-ranging underground tunnels that trip horses and cattle. The capybara is the world's largest rodent, sometimes weighing more than 110 pounds.

Visitors to Patagonia are impressed by the picturesque wildlife of the coasts: dolphins, penguins, and sea lions. The Valdés Peninsula, a large nature reserve on the Atlantic coast, has herds of huge elephant seals, rheas (large ostrich-like birds), guanacos, and many other interesting birds and animals.

Argentinean birds include flamingos, herons, parrots, black-necked swans, and crested screamers. There are also the tinamou, a relative of the ostrich; the albatross, a large, web-footed seabird; and the condor, a huge vulture in danger of extinction.

THE WORLD'S OLDEST DINOSAUR

In November 1989, a scientist from the University of Chicago revealed an amazing discovery. The previous year, in northwestern Argentina, his team had spotted a full skeleton of the most ancient dinosaur yet found. They named it *Herrerasaurus* to honor Victorino Herrera, the goat farmer who led scientists to the bones.

This dinosaur lived 230 million years ago. At that time, scientists believe, most of the earth's land was part of a single supercontinent called Pangaea. This meat-eating dinosaur was about six feet long and weighed 300 pounds. It had sharp teeth like a shark's, talons like an eagle's, and back legs like those of an ostrich.

HISTORY

The first people in Argentina were the Indians of the Americas. They were hunters and food gatherers. Like the Indians of North America, they may have originated from Asia, crossing the Bering Straits from Siberia in prehistoric times.

When the first Europeans arrived, some 300,000 Indians were occupying the land that eventually became Argentina. A combination of war, diseases (such as smallpox and measles), interbreeding, and environmental destruction by the colonists greatly reduced the Indian population. Today, only about 50,000 full-blooded Indians remain.

EXPLORERS ARRIVE

The first European to land in Argentina was reportedly the Portuguese explorer Juan Díaz de Solís, in 1516. He sailed into the Río de la Plata estuary and claimed the land for Spain. (Solís was killed and eaten by Indians at a later landing venture in South America.) Four years later, Portuguese explorer Ferdinand Magellan stopped at the same river on his historic voyage around the world.

In 1527, Sebastian Cabot, an Italian serving Spain, founded the first European settlement, later abandoned, near the present city of Rosario. Cabot named the Río de la Plata, or River of Silver, after the silver jewelry worn by the Indians.

The Cabildo in Buenos Aires. This used to be the council building for the colonial government.

THE COLONIAL PERIOD The history of Argentina is part of the larger story of conquest and subsequent settling of South America by Spanish and Portuguese colonists. The conquest of the Inca Empire of Peru in 1532 by Francisco Pizarro opened the way for these colonists.

Most of the Spaniards who arrived by sea were eventually driven away by the Indians and the threat of starvation. The Spanish colonists who finally settled in Argentina came mainly over the mountains from Peru and Chile. That is how Argentina's oldest cities, such as Jujuy, Salta, Tucumán, Mendoza, and Córdoba, were founded in the latter half of the 16th century. Horses, sheep, and cattle brought from Spain thrived and multiplied in the new land.

During the 17th century, the Spanish government needed money and so sold large plots of land. This led to the establishment of huge estates owned by rich Europeans and *criollos* ("kree-OH-zhos"), or people of European descent born in Latin America. To herd their wild cattle, the owners hired gauchos ("GAH-uh-chos"), or cowboys, who were usually *mestizos* (mes-TEE-zohs"), people of mixed Indian and Spanish blood.

José de San Martín is also known as El Libertador (the liberator) for his leadership in the fight for independence from Spain. His statues dominate the main squares of cities, towns, and villages throughout Argentina. His portrait hangs in every state school and decorates the postage stamps.

INDEPENDENCE

In time, wealthy landowners began to resent the Spanish government's interference in their business affairs. The landowners grew more powerful. They wanted to control trade and keep more of the wealth they produced at home rather than send it back to Spain. They yearned for independence. When France attacked Spain in Europe (1807–08), Buenos Aires seized that opportunity to fight for its independence. On May 25, 1810, Argentina broke away from its mother land, but King Ferdinand of Spain did not recognize the independence of the new colony.

The Argentinean national hero, General José de San Martín (1778–1850), urged Argentinean leaders to formally declare independence from Spain. This happened in Tucumán on July 9, 1816, and the new country was called the United Provinces of the River Plate.

San Martín then led a famous expedition across the Andes into Chile and helped drive out the Spanish troops there and in Peru. Spain's domination of the South American continent finally ended.

FORGING A NATION

The next 50 years were marked by two major forces: the struggle between Buenos Aires and the provinces, and political turmoil under different kinds of government. The *porteños* ("porr-TEH-nyos"), or residents of the port city of Buenos Aires, quarreled with ranchers in the provinces over control of the country's rural areas. These conflicts almost destroyed trade, and in fact the entire economy.

The tyrant Juan Manuel de Rosas—president from 1829 to 1852.

A constitution drawn up in 1826 gave Buenos Aires control over the interior. The first president of Argentina, Bernardino Rivadavia, was a *porteño*. He was soon overthrown by the rival political party of the rural ranchers. Their leader was in turn assassinated by members of Rivadavia's party.

The next ruler was a type that would appear frequently in Argentinean history—the strongman, or *caudillo* ("cow-DEE-zhoh"). Juan Manuel de Rosas (1793–1877), a landowner from the pampas, was dictator of Argentina from 1829 to 1852. He persecuted and murdered many of his political enemies and wiped out a great number of Indians. Rosas was finally overthrown by General Justo José de Urquiza and escaped to England, where he spent the rest of his life in comfortable exile.

THE CONSTITUTION OF 1853

The constitution proclaimed in 1853 was patterned after that of the United States. Urquiza became president of a new confederation of the provinces.

In 1860, Argentina officially adopted its present name, from *argentum,* the Latin word for "silver." The province of Buenos Aires alone refused to join the confederation until 1862, after several battles. Buenos Aires then became the nation's capital, and General Bartolomé Mitre took over as president of the 14 united provinces of the Argentine Republic.

During this period, President Domingo Faustino Sarmiento (1811–1888), who ruled Argentina from 1868 to 1874, vigorously promoted public education in Argentina. To this day, the country has one of the highest literacy rates in the world.

The war between the settlers and the Indians in Tierra del Fuego during the 1880s.

In 1880, Buenos Aires became a federal district, something like the District of Columbia in the United States.

The pressure for more grazing land resulted in the Indian Wars of the late 1870s and early 1880s. During these battles, the Indian tribes in the pampas and Patagonia were virtually exterminated. Their lands were taken over by the officers who led the war against them.

THE GOLDEN AGE

Some historians call the years from 1880 to the outbreak of World War I in 1914 "The Golden Age" of Argentinian history. Huge numbers of immigrants and a great deal of foreign investment arrived from Europe. Argentina—a land of natural resources and frontier wilderness—seemed destined to become one of the world's richest and greatest nations by the early 20th century. The railroad system expanded rapidly. Refrigerated ships began to carry beef and hides to Europe in 1877, and exports of farm products grew rapidly. Sheep farming became more important. By the 1880s, wool constituted half the value of Argentina's exports.

In the early 20th century, Argentina attracted many immigrants, such as the owner of this pharmacy.

During this period, streets were paved, broad avenues and parks were built, and majestic public buildings and private homes sprang up. Argentina became the most urbanized country in Latin America.

In 1929, the Great Depression triggered by the United States stock market crash affected Argentina along with many other countries of the world. As the Argentinean economy declined sharply, army leaders removed the president from office in 1930. A series of military dictatorships ensued. Argentina remained neutral throughout most of World War II (1939–1945). War was finally declared on Germany and Japan in March 1945, a few months before the war ended.

THE PERÓN ERA

The most famous strongman leader in Argentina's history, Colonel Juan Domingo Perón (1895–1974), rose to power while generals ran the government in the 1940s. He served as a minister of labor in a *junta* (group of military leaders) government and then became president in 1946. He appealed to the workers by giving them higher wages, pensions, and other benefits, and by strengthening their unions. His supporters formed the Peronist party, which remains influential to this day.

Before Perón, foreign countries had tremendous power over Argentina's economy. The British controlled most of the railroads. The United States controlled the auto business. Even the meat-packing industry was dominated by foreigners. Perón increased government spending, took control of many of the country's industries, and built up manufacturing at the expense of farm production, which he taxed heavily. The resulting drop in farm production caused the national income to fall.

Civil liberties eroded under Perón. He suspended freedom of the press and freedom of speech, altered the constitution to increase his powers, and permitted a second term of office for himself, not allowed under the 1853 constitution. He remained popular with some Argentineans because of his charm and appeal to their national pride. But during his second term, his power and popularity declined. He lost the support of the Catholic Church and alienated the army and navy. Perón fled in 1955 and eventually settled in Spain, leaving Argentina nearly bankrupt. He left a legacy of huge debts and inflation, yet his ideas continue to appeal to many.

"For people like me, Perón was and still is a prophet, a visionary, a father-figure."

—*Alex Huber*

Juan Domingo Perón.

23

EVITA PERON

Perón's beautiful second wife, Eva Duarte de Perón, known as Evita, a former actress, was a powerful leader in her own right until her early death at 33 from cancer. She was idolized by the urban working class. She gained the right to vote for women in 1947 and founded women's political and social-service organizations. Her work brought health and welfare benefits to the poor. The masses expressed their affection for Evita with huge demonstrations. For many, her magnificent jewels and gowns and her rags-to-riches story symbolized a proud and wealthy Argentina.

Evita was born in the poor village of Los Toldos in 1919. She went to Buenos Aires in her teens and became a popular radio actress. Perón, a widower, was 48 and she was 24 when they met. She greatly assisted his rise to power, and his popularity dropped after her death. Many Argentineans viewed Evita as a near-saint, but the Catholic Church in Rome resisted all pressure to canonize her. Her epitaph reads, "Don't cry for me, Argentina, I remain quite near to you."

DISRUPTION

Military dictators and civilian presidents alternated during the years of Perón's exile. In 1956, Perón's constitution of 1949 was replaced by the original constitution of 1853. Peronists were banned from political activity. The most noted president of this period was Arturo Frondizi (1958–1962), who helped industrialize Argentina. He tried unsuccessfully to lower the national debt and reduce inflation.

After a period of strikes and political unrest, the military allowed a Peronist named Héctor José Cámpora to become president in 1973. Later that year, Perón returned from his Spanish exile. Cámpora resigned, enabling Perón to be elected president once more in October 1973. He governed briefly until his death the following year at the age of 79.

After Perón's death, Isabel, his third wife, became the first woman president. During her term in office, incredible inflation—over 400%—and terrorist violence plagued the country. Kidnappings, bombings, and executions of businessmen, army officers, and newspaper publishers were the work of the left-wing guerrilla group, the *Montoneros* ("mohn-tow-NEH-ros").

After being suppressed by the military dictatorship for many years, the Peronist party returned to power with the support and vote of the people.

THE "DIRTY WAR"

In 1976, military leaders arrested Isabel Perón. They seized the government, dissolved the Congress, outlawed all political parties, censored the press, and banned all strikes. These leaders began a *guerra sucia,* or "dirty war," against the terrorists.

They did succeed in destroying the power of the guerrilla groups, but in their campaign, they condoned violence against thousands. The government often kidnapped and killed many of its enemies as well as innocent people, never revealing their fates.

Mothers and grandmothers of "the disappeared," as they were called, began to demonstrate every Thursday afternoon in the Plaza de Mayo, outside government headquarters. Later investigations revealed that most

Opposite and below: **The Mothers of the Plaza de Mayo. A report published in 1986 lists almost 9,000 cases of people who disappeared during the "dirty war." The real numbers, however, will never be known.**

of the disappeared had been murdered. Hundreds of detention centers had been used around the country to imprison, torture, and kill people. Mass graves were discovered.

A government commission later called the military campaign against the terrorists and dissidents the "greatest tragedy of our history, and the most savage."

27

The Falkland Islands are remote and desolate, inhabited by about 2,000 people in 1984. The island's economy relies solely on sheep farming.

THE FALKLANDS WAR AND DEMOCRACY

Argentina's economy continued to decline, especially during the period of the Falklands War in 1982. Both Britain and Argentina claimed ownership of these islands, which Argentina calls the Islas Malvinas. They lie about 300 miles off the coast of Argentina and the residents are British subjects.

President Leopoldo Galtieri, an army general, had hoped to unite the people behind his military government by occupying these islands. Argentinean troops fought in the air, at sea, and on the islands, but failed to repel the British task force. The Argentinean army never expected such a strong retaliation from Great Britain when they occupied the islands. The war lasted 72 tragic days and took 2,000 Argentinean and British lives.

When Argentina surrendered, it did not give up its claim to the islands. Britain maintains a 2,500-man garrison in the Falklands. It was not until seven years after the war that Argentina and Great Britain resumed consular ties, air and sea links, and unrestricted trade.

This military defeat led to the call for free elections in October 1983. Raúl Alfonsín became president in December of that year and Argentina fully restored the constitution of 1853. Alfonsín tried to bring to justice some of the military commanders who had violated human rights during the "dirty war." Nine commanders were tried, and five received prison sentences. The military was able to prevent the prosecution of lower-ranking officers who, they said, were only following orders.

The short Falklands War further crippled Argentina's weak economy and cost the lives of many British and Argentinean soldiers.

Eventually, economic woes—inflation, unemployment, and falling wages—damaged Alfonsín's popularity. On May 14, 1989, Carlos Saúl Menem of the union-backed Peronist party was elected president. Riots over high food prices led Alfonsín to resign on June 30, allowing Menem to take office five months early.

Menem campaigned as a candidate of a party that traditionally stood for big government, big benefits, and big deficits. Once in office, he surprised his constituents by pushing for freer markets and a reduced role for government. Argentina's high inflation remains his biggest challenge.

GOVERNMENT

ARGENTINA'S official name is República Argentina (Argentine Republic). It was established as a republic on May 1, 1853, when the constitution was adopted. Parts of the Argentinean constitution were modeled after that of the United States. It calls for an elected president and congress. The president and vice-president must be born in Argentina and must be Roman Catholics. They serve a six-year term and cannot be reelected for consecutive terms.

Power is divided between the executive, legislative, and judicial branches of the government. This creates a system of checks and balances that is supposed to prevent one person or branch from gaining complete control of the nation.

The president appoints a cabinet of ministers to head the executive departments of the government. The vice-president leads the Senate and becomes president if the president can no longer serve.

The Congress is made up of two houses, the Chamber of Deputies and the Senate. The larger Chamber of Deputies has 254 members elected directly by the people. Deputies serve for four years. The Senate comprises 46 members chosen by the local legislatures. Two senators come as representatives of each of the 22 provinces, and two come from the Federal District of Buenos Aires. Senators serve for nine years.

In addition to 22 provinces and one federal district, Argentina includes the island territory of Tierra del Fuego. The people in each province can elect a governor, but the president appoints the governor of Tierra del Fuego. The Federal District is run by a mayor appointed by the president. Everyone aged 18 and above can vote in the elections.

Above: **Argentina has two main political parties: the Radical Civic Union or the Radical Party, which attracts many middle-class voters, and the Justicialist Liberation Front, also called the Peronist Party.**

Opposite: **A presidential guard outside the Casa Rosada.**

THE JUDICIARY

The Argentinean system of courts and judges—the judiciary—has been influenced by the systems used in the United States and Western Europe.

The president appoints the members of the Supreme Court and the judges of the Federal Courts of Appeals. All Supreme Court and federal judges are appointed for life.

Each province has its own system of lower and higher courts. Judges in the provinces are appointed by the local governors. Local governments have limited powers, however, due to the fact that the president of Argentina can remove the governor of a province and call for new elections to fill that seat.

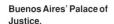
Buenos Aires' Palace of Justice.

The constitution establishes trial by jury for criminal cases, but this is rarely practiced. The death penalty was re-introduced in 1976, more as a deterrent than as punishment, for the killing of government, military police, and judicial officials, and for other terrorist activities. By 1990, it was no longer being used.

THE ARMED FORCES

The president is commander-in-chief of the armed forces. Men from the ages of 18 to 45 must spend 12 months or more in the army or the air force, or a minimum of 14 months in the navy. Women may hold noncombat jobs in the armed forces.

32

At times, the armed forces have been Argentina's strongest political force. Military leaders have made and overthrown governments many times during this century. Some military coups have been bloody, while others were less violent.

No Argentinean president in the 20th century has been able to achieve his goals or even remain in office long without the support of the military. Military takeovers have often affected constitutional governments in Argentina, but only during the "dirty wars" was the constitution actually set aside.

The constitution of 1853 guaranteed the people freedom of speech and religion and gave them the right of public assembly and private property. However, these and other inalienable civil liberties often suffered under military regimes.

The great task in governing Argentina has been to develop a stable government that will not be overthrown whenever it displeases some powerful group in the country, especially the military establishment.

The House of Congress. In a democratic and civilian government, the country's armed forces have reverted to their role of defending the country, not ruling it.

CARLOS SAÚL MENEM

The current president of Argentina, Carlos Saúl Menem, was born in Argentina. He is a Catholic, as required by law, but he comes from a Syrian-Arab Muslim family.

Menem was elected president on May 14, 1989. He belongs to the Justicialist Liberation Front Party. He had been a popular governor of the economically-depressed province of La Rioja in the northwest. As a representative of the Peronist movement, Menem's campaign appealed to the workers and the poor.

Menem often makes headlines because of his flamboyant personality. He has toured Argentina in a luxury bus and been featured in magazines wearing bathing suits. He likes to fly planes and play soccer with the country's leading athletes.

Like the most famous wife of a president in Argentinean history, Evita Perón, Mrs. Menem is a striking blonde. But unlike Evita, Zulema Yoma de Menem is no help to her husband in politics. President Menem and his wife have openly aired their domestic disputes. Newspapers headlined the time when he had her locked out of the official residence. She has publicly voiced her support for Menem's political opponents. Unlike her husband, a Catholic convert, Mrs. Menem retains her Muslim religion.

THE STATE FLAG AND
THE COAT OF ARMS

The sun with a human face, called the "Sun of May," appears on the state flag (adopted in 1818) and on the coat of arms. It represents Argentina's freedom from Spain. The colors, light blue and white, were worn by Argentineans who fought off British invaders in 1806 and 1807.

The coat of arms shows two hands clasped and surrounded by a laurel wreath. In the back is a red "liberty cap" on a pole. On top of the wreath is the rising sun. The light blue and white colors match those of the flag.

ECONOMY

THE SPANISH EXPLORERS named Argentina after the precious silver they were seeking in the new land. But they didn't find much of it. Instead, they brought cattle from Europe and later sheep, and cultivated wheat and other grains. These were the sources of Argentina's economic growth.

Argentina is potentially one of the most prosperous countries in Latin America. Food is plentiful and cheap. The poverty, starvation, and malnutrition that plague many other countries on the continent are virtually unknown in Argentina.

Half of Argentina's total land area is used for pasture. The soil is richly productive in the roughly 12% of the land that is cultivated for crops. The main farm crops include corn, wheat, soybeans, and sorghum. Grapes, apples, citrus fruits, sugarcane, *yerba mate*, tobacco, cotton, and tea are also grown. From the grapes come a variety of wines.

Argentina is famous for its beef production. The British cattle breeds of Aberdeen Angus, Hereford, and Shorthorn, and the French Charolais are particularly popular. Patagonia and other dry areas are key regions for sheep-breeding, with sheep's wool being another major export item. Argentinean farmers raise large numbers of pigs and poultry. The dairy industry is also quite extensive.

About 15% of the work force is employed in agriculture, which accounts for 9% of Argentina's gross national product, or GNP. The GNP measures the total amount of goods and services produced by a country.

Opposite and below: **Early explorers expected to find huge silver deposits in Argentina. The wealth they did find consisted of rich soil and vast stretches of grazing land for cattle.**

Argentina is one of the world's biggest producers and exporters of beef, wool, wine, and wheat.

MANUFACTURING AND SERVICE INDUSTRIES

The manufacturing sector has grown in recent years and accounts for about 36% of Argentina's GNP. Close to one-fifth of the workers are employed in this sector of the economy. Argentina's industrial base is quite diverse, thanks to the bounty of the pampas. The chief industry remains the processing of meat and other food products. Other industries include textiles, leather goods, chemicals, metals, printing, lumber, fishing, automobiles, and railroad cars, plus consumer goods. The country's factories are highly concentrated in and around Buenos Aires.

The service industries produce 55% of Argentina's GNP and employ about 57% of the workforce. Workers in the service sector include those with jobs in the local, state, and federal governments; the military; schools; hospitals; stores; restaurants; and banks. Also of particular importance are workers in the fields of transportation and communications, as their contributions help to build the infrastructure of the economy.

NATURAL RESOURCES

In addition to the rich, fertile soil of the pampas, the country has abundant natural resources. It has enough natural gas reserves to last at least another 60 years. An extensive pipeline system links the natural gas fields with important industrial centers.

Oil and hydroelectric energy sources are being developed. Petroleum supplies about 70% of the energy used in Argentina. The most important oil fields are located in Patagonia and the Piedmont. Argentina is one of the chief oil-producing countries in Latin America. Hydroelectric plants supply about two-fifths of the country's electricity.

Much of Argentina's mineral reserves still remain to be explored. Among the minerals found are beryllium, coal, copper, iron, lead, manganese, tin, tungsten, and zinc.

Although there are large forest reserves, especially in the northeast and the south, the timber industry is still fairly small.

Investment in the development of the nation's resources has led to the recent digging of new quarries, mines, and oil wells. The building of additional roads, dams, and factories has also fostered economic growth, new job opportunities, and the development of the rural areas of the country.

Oil derricks are a common sight in Argentina. The country is self-sufficient in crude petroleum and petroleum products.

Right: Argentina is known for its Quebracho tree, which yields hard wood that can be used as building material and whose extract is used for tanning hides.

Below: Cowhide provides leather from which shoes and jackets are made.

IMPORTS AND EXPORTS

The export of agricultural products provides an excellent balance of trade. Argentina exports about two-thirds more than it imports. Its chief exports are grain, meat, wool, hides, vegetable oils, fruits, vegetables, nuts, and manufactured goods. The countries that receive these goods include the United States, the Russian Federation and other former Soviet republics, Italy, Brazil, Japan, and the Netherlands.

Argentina's chief imports are industrial chemicals, non-electrical machinery, transportation equipment, iron, steel, and coffee. It imports chiefly from the United States, Brazil, Germany, Bolivia, Japan, Italy, and the Netherlands.

To further improve the balance of trade, Argentina strives to increase the production of export goods and to manufacture products locally rather than import them. It produces nearly all the consumer goods—such as cars, refrigerators, and television sets—that it once imported. One potential drawback of this policy is that it misses some opportunities to buy goods that are made more cheaply abroad, where labor costs may be even lower than in Argentina.

INFLATION AND FOREIGN DEBT

The people of Argentina have one of the highest standards of living in South America. Yet other figures tell a story of economic decline. In the 1920s, Argentina had the eighth-largest economy in the world. By 1987, its economy ranked 58th worldwide.

During the Perón era, the government gave the people extensive social welfare services. The social security system provides pensions upon retirement for all workers. It also provides health and maternity benefits, compensation for workers injured on the job, unemployment payments, and financial aid to the poor and the aged.

While these programs seem to help Argentineans live better, many economists blame government spending for the spiraling inflation rate. At times, the government has printed extra money to cover its expenses, thereby increasing inflation.

Through the years of political instability since Perón, the goals of economic productivity and efficiency have been all but ignored. Now state-run industries lose billions of dollars each year.

In 1989, the railroad system lost $2 million a day. The private business sector also depends on subsidies from the government and suffers from "featherbedding," a term meaning that jobs are provided for unproductive workers.

Inflation results in rising costs and a fall in the value of money. This means many people become poorer as their salary and savings drop in value.

41

ARGENTINA IN THE 90S

Despite the problems, Argentineans have grown comfortable with a system in which the government provides jobs for huge numbers of workers and subsidizes many businesses. It would mean a wrenching change for people to give up their guaranteed jobs and cradle-to-grave benefits in order to stabilize the economy.

Argentina faces continuing economic problems. The average annual income in 1991 was $3,100. This low figure is the result, in part, of unemployment and wage controls meant to limit inflation. Inflation soared to a record high of 647% in 1984. Inflation was 83.8% in 1991.

Each year, Argentineans can buy less goods with their income than the year before. With mounting frustration, many Argentineans have watched their wealth decline in recent years. They are living poorly in a country with rich natural resources. Many workers worry about day-to-day economic survival. Some are holding down two or even three jobs to make ends meet. The very wealthy, who make up less than 1% of the population, have different concerns—primarily, fear of losing a lifestyle of luxury based on the government's protection of their special interests. During the years

Buses are slowly replacing railroads, which, in the early part of the 20th century, were used to transport people as well as livestock and agricultural produce to the ports.

of galloping inflation, it is estimated that wealthy Argentineans sent $30 billion to private overseas bank accounts.

At the beginning of the 1990s, Argentineans faced an uncertain economic future. President Menem's government pledged to undertake tough policies geared toward greater economic efficiency. It planned to sell off state enterprises, reduce the number of public jobs, withhold aid from failing private companies, raise prices for basic services, and balance the budget. The government made plans to sell its national telecommunications company and a large part of the national airline to foreign buyers. These sales would wipe out more than US$7 billion of the US$61 billion foreign debt. The transfer of state-owned companies to private owners is a dramatic change in policy from the Peronist party tradition. The Buenos Aires electricity company and some companies owned by the armed forces are due to be sold to private owners, and the national oil company, YPF, has already been privatized.

The stock exchange in Buenos Aires. Argentina, one of the most prosperous countries in South America, is slowly but surely on the road to economic recovery.

ARGENTINEANS

THE HEART OF ARGENTINA is its people, more than 33 million of them.

One of the great surprises for visitors to Argentina is that the people don't look especially "South American." The high cheekbones, darker skin tones, and coal black hair of the native Indian population and the *mestizos* and *mulattos*, or mixed races, are not characteristic of crowds on the street. Instead, these people look European.

Many other countries on the continent have large populations of South American Indians, people of African descent, and mixed races. About 85% of Argentineans, in contrast, are white and of European descent. The remaining 15% are *mestizo*, Indian, and other nonwhite groups.

As people migrated from different parts of Europe, they tended to settle near others from their home country.

Buenos Aires and other large cities and towns still have ethnic neighborhoods where the customs and special foods of European countries are preserved. Some of these groups publish newspapers in their own languages. They also run schools, hospitals, and clubs for their countrymen.

Another surprise to visitors is that the largest group comes not from Spain but from Italy. About four out of 10 people in Argentina are of Italian descent, while only about three out of 10 trace their families back to Spain. Most of the Italian immigrants settled in and around Buenos Aires.

Opposite:**The gauchos were once despised as being hard-drinking and rowdy. Today, they have come to represent the admirable qualities of an Argentinean: nobility, courage, and independence.**

Below: **Unlike children from other South American countries, these toddlers have very European features.**

OTHER ETHNIC ROOTS

Argentina once had the largest community of British people anywhere in the world outside Britain. British expatriates were influential in developing the country's railway, telephone, electricity, gas, and steamship services.

They brought sports such as rugby, cricket, polo, and tennis, and imported cattle from England. Today their descendants are called Anglo-Argentines. The Falklands War between Great Britain and Argentina presented them with a potential conflict of loyalties, but most sided with Argentina.

The lure of new land has not dimmed. More than one million Europeans came following World War II. Europe's loss was Argentina's gain. Along with the numerous Italian, Spanish, English, and Welsh immigrants, Argentina was also enriched by people of Austrian, Dutch, French, German, Irish, Jewish, Polish, Portuguese, Russian, Swiss, Chinese, Japanese, and Syrian descent. Immigrants have also come from neighboring South American countries, largely for political and economic reasons. Most recently, newcomers have arrived from Southeast Asia.

Argentina's people come mostly from Italy, Spain, France, Russia, Germany, Britain, and Poland.

SOCIAL CLASSES

When the major waves of European immigrants arrived in Argentina, they found that the rural areas were controlled by large landowners. The newcomers could not easily own land or houses in the countryside, so they went instead to the major cities, especially to Buenos Aires.

The cities enabled immigrants to find jobs, gain an education, and become part of Argentina's middle class. For this reason, Argentina has a larger middle class than most other Latin American countries. The urban middle class includes workers in small businesses, as well as some government officials and professionals.

From the mid-18th century to the mid-19th century, political and social life in Argentina were shaped by the "landed aristocracy." These were the large rural landowners. Many had close ties to Britain and its culture. Wealthy members of the upper class considered themselves among the world's most sophisticated, well traveled and best educated people.

In the past, the landed aristocracy held most power. Now urban leaders of industry, commerce, and the professions, and military officers exercise considerable power in determining how the country is run. Social divisions are based on money, education, and family background. Hence a certain amount of snobbery exists.

Since the 1930s, large numbers of people have left the countryside to seek work in Argentina's larger cities. Many found only part-time work and have become part of a poor lower class that live in slum conditions.

Among the wealthy today are ranchers, or *estancieros* ("ess-tahn-see-EH-ros"), who own large tracts of land and herds of cattle but live in the cities. They work their farms and ranches with their families, and perhaps with the help of a few hired hands.

THE PROUD GAUCHOS

The gauchos ("GAH-oo-chohs") are a special group of men in Argentina who used to roam the pampas on horseback. Most were *mestizos*. A much smaller number still work as ranch hands on cattle ranches today. The gauchos of the past have become folk heroes and continue to inspire the culture of the country as a symbol of strength and individualism.

Like the cowboys of the North American West, the gauchos were excellent horsemen. They tamed wild horses, herded cattle, and were skilled and courageous. They could find their way on the plains under any circumstances. By chewing grass, they could tell whether there was water nearby and whether it was salted or fresh. They could tell directions from the lay of the grass, or count the number of riders by their sound alone.

One costume that the world associates with Argentina is the dress of the gauchos. They are known for their thick leather belts, decorated with silver and sometimes with old coins.

Gauchos often led rugged lives with few comforts. They lived in huts with mud walls and floors, a straw roof, no windows, and, frequently, an animal hide for a door. They were proud, self-reliant, and tough. They fought for survival against the forces of nature and the Indians. During colonial times, they opposed the authority of Spain. Later, they lived in opposition to the new settlers who fenced-in the open range.

During the 19th century, their main job was to take cattle to the markets in Buenos Aires. The building of roads and railroads and the fencing-in of the *estancias* ("ess-TAHN-see-ahs") changed all that. Today, the gauchos still work on the open range driving tractors, repairing engines, and vaccinating cattle against disease.

Gauchos adopted the use of *bolas* ("BOH-lahs") from the Indians. A *bola* is a long rope ending in two or three pieces tied to hard balls covered with leather. They are used for fighting and hunting, especially when pursuing the ostrich-like rhea. When thrown, a *bola* wraps around the legs of a running animal and trips and ties them up. Several times a year, during rodeos, one can watch gauchos exhibiting their legendary horsemanship skills. The gauchos survived on a diet of meat and *yerba mate*, a holly tea. A typical picture of a gaucho shows him on horseback or at rest, singing and accompanying himself with a guitar, or sipping *yerba mate* from a hollowed-out gourd through a metal straw.

THE CRIOLLOS

In colonial times, the word *criollos* ("kree-OH-yhos") meant people born in Argentina to Spanish parents. Later, it came to mean descendants of the early Spanish settlers, as opposed to families of 19th century European immigrants. Today, it can also mean a person who lives in the country or in a small town. The *criollos* who worked the land have provided much wealth for the country.

49

ANCIENT INDIAN TRADITIONS

The roughly 50,000 pure-blooded Argentinean Indians in Argentina tend to live in the isolated areas of the Andes, the Gran Chaco, Patagonia, and Tierra del Fuego. The Diaguita Indians, for example, live west of Salta at 9,800 feet. This area was part of the Inca empire before the Spaniards arrived in the 16th century.

Although the soil is poor, the Indians farm the mountainsides, growing beans, corn, and potatoes. They use irrigation channels built centuries ago by their ancestors to help in their farming.

Because the air is too thin at this altitude for cattle and

sheep to live, these Indians use llamas for meat, wool, and transportation. From the llama wool, the women weave clothing for their families, and socks, sweaters, scarves, and blankets to sell to tourists.

Each Indian community has its own style of dress. Women's hairstyles also differ from one region to the next. The Diaguita people observe a mixture of Argentinean and traditional tribal customs.

Christianity merges here with ancestral beliefs. These Indians pray to gods of the sun, the moon, the earth, and also to the gods of thunder, rain, and lightning.

Opposite above: **This Indian man has hunted and killed a *gila* monster. The Indians in Argentina remain economically backward as the lands within the Indian reservations are mostly barren.**

Opposite below: **An Indian girl. The Indians have the distinctively Asian features of their ancestors who crossed the Bering Straits to North America.**

DISAPPEARANCE OF BLACKS

Argentina had a significant black population in its early years. These were the descendants of slaves imported from Africa by the Spanish in the 16th century. Argentineans of African descent constituted about 30% of Buenos Aires' population beginning in 1778.

These people were slaves until the slave trade was outlawed in 1813. Most slaves were freed by 1827, but some didn't attain freedom until 1861. After the emancipation, most blacks continued to suffer from low status in Argentinean society.

Between 1836 and 1887, the percentage of blacks in Buenos Aires dropped from 26% to 1.8%. Historical paintings, prints, and photographs and the epic poem *Martín Fierro* revealed the presence of these Afro-Argentines, who are rarely seen today. Their disappearance from Argentina's society remains something of a mystery.

Some scholars believe that the majority of blacks died during the yellow fever epidemic of 1871, or in warfare, or disappeared through interbreeding with white colonists.

LIFESTYLE

THE ARGENTINEAN PEOPLE are still in the process of evolving a more unified culture. Their relatively short history of immigration trends resulted in many Argentineans keeping to the family customs brought from their country of origin. Also, the great variations in geography called for various ways of coping with life. The Welsh sheep-ranchers of Patagonia, the Indian farmers of the Andes, and the city sophisticates of Buenos Aires could not be more different from each other. For these reasons, there are many different lifestyles in Argentina.

Yet certain customs and traits are shared by most Argentineans: they are strongly nationalistic; they are pretty relaxed about punctuality; and they love to talk sports—especially soccer—and politics.

"The Argentines are still trying to figure out if they're European or Latin American, and they are famous throughout Latin America for not having made up their minds yet."

—*Deirdre Ball*

Opposite: **An extensive cafe culture similar to that of southern Europe forms a big part of Argentinean life.**

Left: **A little girl feeds pigeons in the park.**

53

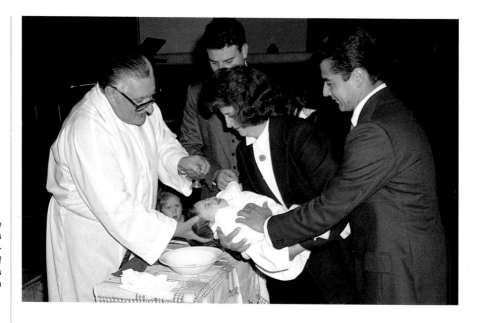

FROM BIRTH TO DEATH

The traditions and customs of any society are usually influenced by religion. The majority of Argentinean Catholics follow the practices of the church in observing important events in their lives.

Babies are usually baptized, and first communion is celebrated around the age of seven or eight. Girls have their first dancing party with boys when they are 15. This is society's recognition that they are now old enough to date.

When a couple becomes engaged to be married, they exchange rings. The woman wears her ring on the fourth finger of the right hand until the wedding, when she shifts it to her left hand. In the wedding ceremony, the groom walks in with his mother and the bride with her father. This custom symbolizes that both are leaving their families and joining as man and wife at the altar.

When people die, their bodies may be either buried or cremated. It is quite unusual for the body of a dead person to be embalmed and viewed in an open coffin, as was done for Evita Perón.

FAMILY LIFE

Family life is very important to Argentineans. Families tend to be nurturing and supportive, and Argentineans love to hear compliments about their home and children. This close bond among family members makes them fiercely loyal to one another.

Children are rarely sent away to boarding school; they are quite likely to live at home until marriage and then settle near their parents. University students generally attend classes in their hometown and continue to live with their parents. Workers often come home for lunch.

People care for their elderly parents and frequently invite a widowed parent to live with them. It is not common for the elderly to live in nursing homes.

The most outstanding traits of an Argentinean include a close bond with family and place of birth, a strong sense of patriotism, and a profound respect for tradition and culture.

The extended family of aunts, uncles, and cousins have frequent reunions. This network of connections is often used to gain social advantages by getting into a better school or gaining a better job.

The father is often a strong authoritarian figure in the family. He also bears the chief responsibility for earning money to support the family, although many women also work and contribute to the family's income.

Young people live under the rules of their families and may feel controlled by them through their teen years and often until marriage or even later.

Right and below: **The fashion-conscious look to Europe and to a lesser extent the United States for the latest trends in clothing and makeup.**

CITY LIFESTYLE

The history of Argentina is marked by the contrast and sometimes the conflict between city and rural people. In many ways, they have opposing views of life.

City life in Argentina reflects the European roots of an immigrant nation. The architecture and city plan—the layout of streets, parks, and squares—have a European look. As in Spanish cities, the cathedrals and chief government buildings are found facing the plaza, or main square. Argentina's artistic culture, organization of schools, fashion, business customs, and forms of polite behavior are very European.

The Buenos Aires *porteños* are the leading city dwellers in Argentina. They dominate its government and cultural life. *Porteños* view themselves as sophisticated and up-to-date, and frequently set trends in behavior and fashion that later spread to the provinces.

Many *porteños* have little interest in visiting other parts of Argentina. They sometimes feel superior to people from the countryside and are accused of viewing anyone who doesn't live in Buenos Aires as one of the *campesinos* or country folk, even if that person happens to live in another big city.

FRIENDSHIP THRIVES IN THE CAFE

Argentineans love to discuss sports, politics, philosophy, and the arts. In Buenos Aires, particularly, this means lingering in a cafe talking with friends. There are hundreds of old cafes that spill onto the busy streets. What one orders is less important than the relaxed atmosphere. The waiters never rush the customers. The English custom of tea-time and snacks in the afternoon continues in Argentina.

The Tortoni is the oldest traditional cafe in Buenos Aires, founded in 1858. It has a charming old billiard room, and the walls are decorated with presents from painters and writers who have gathered there over many decades. Conspirators and army chiefs have also come to sip coffee or play a game of chess. Jazz performances add to the attractions on weekends.

Cafes, restaurants, and clubs stay open very late. The typical workday runs from 9 a.m. to 7 p.m., or even as late as 10 p.m. Dinner may be eaten at 10 p.m., or as late as midnight. Some streets of Buenos Aires are bustling with people long after the clock strikes 12.

Because Argentineans are often creatures of habit, many prefer to meet over and over again at the same familiar cafe. Bookstores offer a popular alternative meeting place for intellectuals. The favorite discussion, always, is what it means to be Argentinean.

Opposite above: **A country house by the sea.**

Opposite below: **In the mountainous and hilly regions, horses are still a common means of transportation.**

THE SUGAR, SALT, AND SPICE OF RELATIONSHIPS

The warmth of family ties is extended to friends. People tend to touch each other often when meeting together. They hug and kiss on meeting and leaving one another. When introduced, men shake hands, but close male friends may hug one another in greeting. Women who are friends shake hands with both hands and kiss one another on both cheeks.

Argentine flirting has a certain style. A man may pass a woman on the street and compliment her on her beauty without expecting her to stop or reply. His compliment, called a *piropo*, may be indirect: "It must be lonely in heaven since one of the more beautiful angels has descended to earth!" Less poetically, when passing a mature woman, the man might say: "Old but still good."

Women also flirt, making witty remarks and even put-downs that are meant to be heard and enjoyed by other friends. It has been said that, "in the United States, women are called sweet; in Spain, they are called salty; but in Argentina, women are spicy."

COUNTRY LIFESTYLE

In the interior, European influences on lifestyle are less noticeable. There are many ways of living in the country. Some people in the countryside live and work on huge ranches, often built as luxurious country estates in the Spanish style of architecture. Others live on small farms. The poorest people live in homes made of straw and mud with dirt floors.

Country people tend to see themselves as humbler, having more common sense, and being in better touch with the land than the people of the cities. They sometimes resent what appears to them to be the self-centered arrogance of the *porteños*.

The great rivalry between the people of the interior and the people of Buenos Aires, once so heated, no longer erupts into violence. The two different ways of life are today increasingly seen as complementary to one another.

Above and below: **The rich live in luxurious houses, while the poor live in overcrowded shanty towns known as** *villa miserias.*

RICH AND POOR

Another major contrast is between the lifestyles of the wealthy in Buenos Aires' northern suburbs and the poor who live in slums a mere bus ride away. Church and volunteer organizations have joined together to raise money to build adequate housing for the shanty town residents of Tigre, a fading resort northwest of the city.

Charitable giving runs counter to the Argentinean tradition of avoiding taxes and other obligations to society. In the past, people saw too much of their funds disappear into bribes, payments to unnecessary "middle men," and theft. Hence the volunteers need to assure wealthy donors that the money they give will truly reach the people it is intended to help.

POLITICAL TALK

Under the recent democratic governments, the Argentinean people have resumed their enthusiastic public displays of their political views.

In 1945, thousands of workers answered Evita Perón's call to protest her husband's detention by marching in the Plaza de Mayo. Historians mark that event as the day the working class gained real political power.

Street rallies, marches, and people carrying placards are part of the traditional expression of political ideas in Argentina. Traffic halts for union demonstrators and students playing protest songs. Political graffiti can be found on many buildings and walls.

During elections, Argentineans will turn out in large numbers to vote at the polls. Most speak freely about which political party they support and who they voted for in the last elections.

A street rally in Buenos Aires.

Below: **Women surgeons are more common in today's climate of sexual equality.**

Opposite, above: **A woman sells jewelry from a street stall.**

Opposite, below: **Weight-lifting is an untraditional way for women to keep fit.**

WOMEN

Traditionally, women in Argentina do not play a large role in public life. Evita Perón is especially admired by many feminists for her active role in promoting the rights of women. She worked to gain womens' right to vote, and she advocated many rights for women workers.

Through her efforts, divorce was made legal, but this right was withdrawn shortly after her husband's fall in 1955. Not until 1987 was divorce legalized again.

Women have equal rights under the constitution. Since the 1940s, they

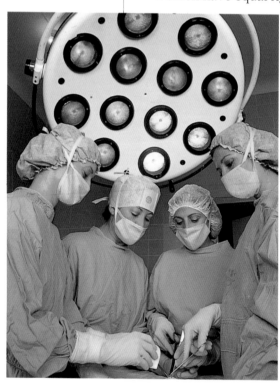

have become more active working outside the home. Women work as doctors, lawyers, architects, and in other professions. President Juan Perón's third wife, Isabel, became president of the country. But still, women are a long way from enjoying an equal role with men in business and government.

Women became forceful in public life during the "dirty war," when the courageous "Mothers of the Plaza de Mayo" marched each Thursday past the Casa Rosada carrying placards inscribed with the names of their missing loved ones. At great personal risk, they demonstrated to end human rights abuses and hold the government accountable for the "disappeared."

When a woman marries, she keeps her maiden name. If María García marries Juan Adler, she becomes María García de Adler or Senora García de Adler.

Letters are addressed not to "Mr. and Mrs. Juan Adler" but to "Mr. Juan Adler and Mrs.," which reads in Spanish *"Señor Juan Adler y Señora."* Children take the father's last name.

Although it is acceptable for women to go to restaurants and theaters without a chaperone, women more commonly go out in groups or accompanied by a man.

Physical abuse of women is not culturally acceptable in Argentina. Crimes of rape and incest are considered rare and are not frequently reported to doctors or police.

Teenage pregnancies and illegitimate children are also uncommon. Although it is a Catholic country, the knowledge and practice of contraception and abortion is common in Argentina.

ARGENTINEAN ATTITUDES

While some Argentineans go in for dramatic gestures, the general tendency is to avoid loud and unusual behavior in public. They don't like to call too much attention to themselves. Still, they may show their emotions, both happiness and sadness, with a Latin American openness of expression.

A leisurely schedule governs the gatherings of friends. People invited for dinner arrive 30 to 60 minutes after the specified time. When invited to a birthday party, guests bring gifts, which are usually opened in their presence.

Many Argentineans go to psychiatrists or psychoanalysts, and many of the analysts in Spain come from Argentina.

Some think psychiatry is popular because people see themselves more as individuals than as part of a group. They tend to be quite concerned with their personal thoughts and feelings.

When you ask for directions on the street, an Argentinean may give a detailed (and possibly wrong) answer rather than admit that he or she doesn't know. It's a point of pride for some people to appear to know the right answer.

Some dramatize their lives or cover up their poverty with a bit of exaggeration. A woman may tell her friends that her car and driver brought her to the restaurant where they are meeting for lunch when, in truth, she came on the bus. A man may tell a new acquaintance that he lives in a building known for its expensive apartments when he actually lives in a more modest home.

As in other countries, Argentineans have ways of attracting good luck. One tango dancer, for example, crosses herself and prays that each performance will be successful. Some performers wear lucky amulets or put on the same tie whenever they go on stage.

The people of Argentina are very open about their feelings and emotions, though they are more conservative than other South Americans.

Right: **Telephone wires are not hidden underground but are exposed overhead. In the financial district of Buenos Aires, so many telephone lines are strung together that they resemble a giant cobweb spreading above the city streets.**

Below: **Nightlife in Buenos Aires. Many restaurants in the cities are open until the early hours of the morning.**

SOCIAL AND BUSINESS CUSTOMS

Argentineans prefer to do business in person rather than over the phone. Appointments for business meetings are preferred to unexpected visits to an office.

It is polite to make small talk at the end of a business meeting, rather than leave abruptly when things are settled. Most Argentineans prefer not to discuss business during meals. The pace of negotiations is much slower than in the United States, for example, and is based more on personal contact.

Many people drop in on friends from around 4 to 6 p.m. without calling

NOSTALGIA FOR THE PAST

Argentineans are said to have a sentimental streak. They remember the past in songs and stories, and in the glorification of the gaucho as a folk hero. The architecture of the cities is full of reminders of the past—old fountains, wrought-iron gates, and countless other details. Families remember their immigrant past through collections of treasured photographs. Tango music expresses this nostalgia with lyrics that speak of lost loves and unfulfilled dreams.

ahead. Social plans are likely to be spontaneous, rather than scheduled weeks in advance.

Especially in Buenos Aires, people stay out late many nights of the week and seem to survive on little sleep. Shops are closed on Saturday afternoon so that people may rest to prepare themselves for Saturday night activities. Shops are also closed on Sunday, and families commonly gather for large noon meals.

RELIGION

ROMAN CATHOLICISM is the official religion of Argentina. The vast majority of the people, more than 90%, call themselves Catholic, yet less than 20% attend church regularly. In general, the people take a relaxed view toward religion. Still, when the Pope visited in 1982 and again in 1987, millions flocked to see the spiritual leader.

According to the constitution of 1853, the president and vice-president must be Roman Catholics. The government also provides some financial support for the Church. The constitution guarantees freedom of religion for all people and requires that strong relations exist between the Church and the state, but in an environment of religious pluralism and freedom.

Each religious group can maintain its own churches, hospitals, social centers, and cemeteries. Religious schools are allowed, but religion may not be taught in the public schools. Religious faiths or sects can be banned if they appear to threaten public order and morality.

By law, all children must be registered at birth with names, usually biblical, that are in a registry of acceptable first names. These are often but not always names of Catholic saints in the Spanish language.

Within the Catholic Church are different groups, or orders, that do different kinds of work. Some run hospitals, some guide education, some try to convert non-Catholics, and some work with prisoners. In religious matters, monks and priests follow the direction of local bishops, who are guided by the Vatican.

Opposite: **There are many church buildings, grand and simple, in Argentina. Small town churches around the country are modeled after Spanish chapels.**

Below: **The grand and opulent architecture of the colonial churches bears testimony to the past wealth and power of the church.**

Above: An Armenian wedding. Racial and religious intolerance is not characteristic of the Argentinean people, as they originate from a diversity of different cultures.

Below: A vodoo ritual in progress.

Above: An Armenian wedding. Racial or religious intolerance is not characteristic of the Argentinean people as they themselves were from diverse and different cultures.

Below: A vodoo ritual in progress.

OTHER RELIGIOUS GROUPS

About 2% of the population today are Protestants. Besides Roman Catholics and Protestants, there are Christians belonging to the Armenian, Orthodox, and Ukrainian Catholic churches. Many Jews came from Europe in the late 19th and early 20th centuries. They number less than 2% of the population and live mostly in Buenos Aires. Muslims, spiritualists, sect members, and atheists make up about 1.3% of the population.

Writers have called the reverence paid to Evita Perón a kind of religious fervor. After her death, her husband tried unsuccessfully to have her made a saint by the Catholic Church. Her followers still place fresh flowers at her tomb every day. Believers ask her to grant their wishes and protect them from harm.

Religion is especially strong in the rural areas. The *mestizo* descendants of immigrants retain elements of anamistic Indian religions mixed with Roman Catholic beliefs and practices. They pray to spirits in nature as well as to the Christian God. They have festivals throughout the year dedicated to the Indian gods; parties are filled with singing, dancing, and feasting. Folk religion, blended at times with superstition, thrives away from Buenos Aires. Local shrines to unofficial saints are popular sites for pilgrimages.

About six weeks before Easter, at the beginning of the period called Lent, the yearly celebration of Carnival begins. In parts of Argentina, the decorations for Carnival are inspired as much by folk religion as by Christianity. Superstition blends with Christianity, for example, when a person makes the sign of the cross to ward off the "evil eye." Magical, occult, and "new age" spiritualism have found expression in Argentina too.

Christ of the Andes. Situated on the Argentinean-Chile border, the statue was erected to symbolize the lasting peace between the two countries.

YAMANA BELIEFS

The Yamana Indians, now extinct, were an ancient aboriginal people who lived at the southern tip of Argentina. Their stories were passed down orally but were never put in writing until a priest, Father Martin Gusinde, collected their legends from the last survivors in the 1920s. Myths about their people include a story of a great flood.

Lexuwakipa, a spirit-woman in the form of an ibis-bird, felt offended by the people. In revenge, she made it snow so much that a huge mass of ice covered the earth. When it started to melt, it flooded the earth. The glaciation occurred at the time when men battled women and succeeded in seizing their secret meeting place, which was the source of the women's power.

The water rose steadily and rapidly, and the people tried to save themselves. Finally, only five mountain peaks remained above water. After the water remained level for two full days, it subsided. Practically all the Yamana had drowned. Only a few families managed to save themselves. Once the great flood had subsided, those few survivors began to rebuild their homes. But ever since that time, the men have ruled the women.

MIRACULOUS STATUES

Incredible tales about miraculous statues abound among Argentina's churches. Here are two of the more famous examples.

THE VIRGIN OF LUJÁN In 1630, before the town of Luján existed, a man tried to drive an oxcart carrying a statue of the Virgin Mary over the place where the church now stands. But it would not move.

THE DEAD CORREA AND NEW BEGINNINGS

A cult has grown around the legend of The Dead Correa (*La Difunta Correa*). The story tells of a starving woman who crossed the desert on foot in search of her husband, a soldier. She died of thirst, but her baby was found alive, sucking at her breast.

The Dead Correa is the unofficial patron saint of new beginnings. In little roadside shrines to her memory, people leave bottles of water. When the water evaporates, they say it has been drunk by the Dead Correa. Thousands of pilgrims visit her shrine in western Argentina near San Juan during Holy Week. While some dress in black mourning clothes, others bring offerings, such as wedding dresses, that reflect their answered prayers.

No matter how many oxen were hitched to the cart, the statue would still not move. The people decided that the Virgin Mary did not want her statue to leave that spot.

They unloaded it and built a small chapel for it. A large, richly decorated church was later built for the thousands of pilgrims who came to Luján each year to pray to the Virgin. Luján is about 44 miles west of Buenos Aires.

THE CRUCIFIX OF SALTA In the 17th century, a statue of Christ on the cross was being shipped to Salta Cathedral from Spain when the ship carrying it sank in a storm at sea. Miraculously, the statue floated to the coast of Peru. It was then carried by a horse across the Andes to Salta, a distance of 1,600 miles.

There were great celebrations when the statue arrived safely. After the festivities it was packed and stored away in the cathedral cellar.

A hundred years later, a major earthquake shook Salta. The people went to the cathedral to pray. They heard a voice saying that the earthquake would not stop until the statue was put in its proper place in the cathedral. The statue was brought out and paraded around the city before being returned to the cathedral. The earthquake stopped. Since then, the statue has been paraded around the city each year to celebrate the event.

LA NACION
La Justicia ordenó no publicar una solicitada
Se celebran hoy los 177 años de la gesta de Mayo

LANGUAGE

JUST ABOUT EVERYBODY in Argentina speaks Spanish, the official language of the country. Spanish is taught in virtually all the schools and is the only language used by the government.

The Spanish used throughout Argentina is full of local variations. Some dialects are so different from the Spanish spoken in Spain that people from both places have trouble understanding one another.

The large number of people who immigrated from Italy have changed the language greatly, giving an Italian sound to the pronunciation of some words and adding other words from the Italian language. The Italian influence is most noticeable around Buenos Aires and in the pampas, where many Italians settled. The Italian greeting *buongiorno* often replaces *buenos días*, the Spanish hello. Goodbye becomes *chau*, a variation of the Italian *ciao* (pronounced "chow").

The *mestizos* in the north use dialects influenced by Indian languages, though generally Indian languages have less of an influence in Argentina than in many other South American countries. The descendents of immigrants from Mexico, Bolivia, Chile, and Paraguay speak in their own distinctive Spanish dialects.

Above: **Argentinians love to chat while having a drink.**

Opposite: **Reading is a favorite pastime and newspapers, books, and magazines can be easily purchased everywhere.**

The many immigrants and Indian tribes have lent great variety to the local dialects used in Argentina.

OTHER VOICES

English is spoken throughout Argentina as a second language. Other languages, such as German, are still spoken by immigrants in the larger towns and cities. Welsh is spoken by descendants of the Welsh immigrants in Patagonia.

Only a small number of the remaining Indians in Argentina still speak Guaraní, Quechua, or other Indian languages. The names of these disappearing languages are quite musical: Aymará, Chiriguano, Chorotí, Mataco, Mocoví, Toba, Lule, Ranquel, Moleche, Tehuelche, and Ona. Scholars are beginning to preserve the legends and traditions that will disappear when the people who speak these languages die out.

OF GANGSTERS AND TANGO SINGERS

A special language related to tango music, popular songs, and the theater is called *lunfardo* ("loon-FAR-doh"). This dialect has influenced the Spanish spoken in Buenos Aires since around 1900. *Lunfardo* uses words borrowed from Italian, Portuguese, and many other languages.

Lunfardo began as a form of criminal slang. Words were borrowed, invented, and used in a way that could only be understood by people who used the dialects. *Lunfardo* playfully changes the names of things. For instance, to speak of a person's head, the *lunfardo* speaker might choose words that mean "a bed of fleas," "thinker," "ball," or "the top of a building."

Soon poets and journalists discovered the colorful expressions of *lunfardo* and began to use them in their writing. Tango singers also began to use them in their songs. From 1916, poets wrote works in *lunfardo* with such titles as *Versos Rantifusos* (Street Verses) and *La Crencha Engrasada* (Slicked-Down Hair). The first tango to be sung had *lunfardo* lyrics and was called *Mi Noche Triste* (My Night of Grief). It was sung in 1917 by Carlos Gardel, the most famous of all tango singers.

For a period of time beginning in the 1940s, the government banned *lunfardo.* Nevertheless, it continued to enrich the spoken and written language of Buenos Aires. As with all slangs, new words were added and old ones dropped over the years. In 1962, a group of scholars, artists, and radio people founded the Lunfardo Academy of Buenos Aires to preserve and polish this distinctive language.

A tango singer expresses himself in the language of the *lunfardo.*

DID YOU KNOW...?

The Argentinean people tend to speak quickly and pronounce some consonants differently from the Spaniards in Europe. Some "s" sounds in Argentina are pronounced "th" in Spain. The Castilian Spanish of Spain sounds almost as if the speaker is lisping to a person used to the sounds of the English language. In Argentina, the "ll" sound is like a soft "j" or "sh." In other Spanish-speaking South American countries such as Chile, "ll" sounds like a "y."

When Spanish is written, question marks (?) and exclamation marks (!) appear not only at the end of a sentence, but also placed upside down before the first word.

In Spanish, the meaning of a word can change depending on which syllable is stressed. *Papá*, with the stress on the last syllable, means father. *Papa* with no stress on the final syllable means potato.

There is no a.m. or p.m. in the Spanish language. To say 8 a.m., a speaker must use words that translate as eight in the morning. Airports and train and bus stations usually use a 24-hour clock. For example, when it is 3 p.m., these clocks read "15:00."

ARGENTINEANS LOVE TO READ

With their country's high literacy rate, Argentineans read many newspapers in Spanish and in foreign languages. At least 230 newspapers are published, about 70 in Buenos Aires alone. *La Prensa,* known for its excellent coverage of international news, and *La Nación,* are two important dailies, each over 120

Spanish-speaking tourists may find it difficult to understand the local Spanish spoken on the streets.

years old. Newspapers published in Buenos Aires are sold in most of the country. Major provincial cities also have their own newspapers. The oldest in print is probably *La Capital,* founded in Rosario in 1867.

The degree of freedom enjoyed by the press has varied under different political regimes. *La Prensa* was seized by Juan Perón's officials in 1949 and was not returned to its owners until 1955. Publications have been banned because they were considered immoral or pro-communist by the government. In 1976, a period of book censorship began, and scholars were persecuted for their ideas. The present government allows the press and writers freer expression of ideas and criticisms.

The *Buenos Aires Herald,* founded in 1876, is the most important English-language newspaper in South America. One of the best in non-English-speaking countries, it is sold in several cities in Argentina.

Colorful streetside stalls selling magazines and newspapers are a common sight in the cities.

More than 4,000 publications are published each year in Argentina. The first magazine, *La Ilustración Argentina,* was printed in 1853. Picture magazines such as *Gente* and *Siete Días* are very popular. Among the best-known literary magazines are *Ficción, Sur,* and *Nosotros.* Readers browse in the country's 8,000 bookstores, many of which are open 24 hours a day.

RADIO AND TELEVISION

Argentina has more than 100 radio stations and numerous television stations. Buenos Aires alone has four television stations: three state-owned and one private. It is estimated that there is one radio in use for every 1.5 persons and one television set for every 5.2 persons. In comparison, the averages for the United States are two radios per person and one television per 1.7 persons. Many television programs are imported from the United States and dubbed in Spanish.

EDUCATION AND LITERACY

Almost everyone in Argentina can read and write as schooling has been made compulsory for all children.

Argentina has an astonishing 94% literacy rate. Education is free from kindergarten to university. Children attend seven grades of elementary education. This requirement is generally obeyed, even in rural areas where schools are hard to reach.

The school year runs from March to December in most parts of the country. Lessons are taught in Spanish, but English, French, and Italian are taught from elementary school onwards. Elementary students may wear white coats over their own clothes. In many junior high schools, the students wear uniforms.

Although high school education is not compulsory, there are free government schools plus private schools in most big towns and cities. They offer five years of classes. Only a small percentage of students finish secondary school.

There are more than 50 public and private universities. The University of Buenos Aires is the largest, with more than 100,000 students. The University of Córdoba is Argentina's oldest, founded in 1613. Because many students work full-time, night courses are quite popular. The three most popular subjects are architecture, political science, and medicine.

Public schools largely owe their success to President Domingo Faustino Sarmiento (1811–1888). He enlisted the advice of a famous United States educator, Horace Mann. However, Argentina's public school system was modeled closely after the French system. These schools later helped to "Argentinize" the children of immigrants.

PROVERBS WITH A SPANISH TWIST

Some proverbs take on a different flavor in a different language. Here are some English proverbs and the English translations of the Spanish versions:

- English : Too many cooks spoil the broth.
  Spanish : A ship directed by many pilots soon sinks.
- English : Don't count your chickens before they're hatched.
  Spanish : Don't eat the sausages before you kill the pig.
- English : A bird in the hand is worth two in the bush.
  Spanish : A bird in the hand is worth a hundred flying.
- English : You cannot make a silk purse out of a sow's ear.
  Spanish : You can't find pears on an elm tree.
- English : Much ado about nothing.
  Spanish : Much noise (of cracking), few nuts.

(SOURCES: *Native Tongues* by Charles Berlitz and *La Illustración Argentina*.)

ARTS

IF THE HEART of Argentina is its people, the soul of the country is its artistic culture. Outstanding artists have created works of international interest in dance, music, drama, literature, painting, sculpture, and architecture. Argentina's creative center is the greater Buenos Aires region. *Porteños* support fine museums, theaters, art galleries, plus opera, symphony, and dance companies. The larger cities also have thriving libraries, museums, theaters, and concert halls.

Argentinean art often reflects international styles and ideas. Churches, homes, and civic buildings recall their counterparts in Spain, Italy, and France. Much popular music pays homage to jazz, pop, and rock music from the United States.

The outside world has long recognized the power and originality of Argentinean artists. They have persisted through periods of political repression, some forced into exile while others courageously continued to work in their homeland. The return of democracy to the country in the 1980s sparked a cultural revival in all the arts.

Partly because there are few Indians to influence the culture of Argentina, folk arts and crafts are not as prominent as in other South American countries. A blend of Indian and Spanish traditions shape the woodcarvings, bolos, ponchos, *mate* (tea) sets, handwoven fabrics, hammocks, costume jewelry, and other handicrafts produced today.

Opposite: **Everybody knows Argentina to be the Land of the Tango.**

Below: **Paintings for sale in a market. Argentinean artists are very influenced by European art.**

ART THROUGH ARGENTINEAN EYES

NATIVE ART The earliest artistic expressions to be found in Argentina are cave paintings and engravings, some small stone heads, and a carving of a human foot with six toes.

The archeological remains and pre-Columbian menhirs—tall stone columns—in Tafí del Valle in Tucumán province are particularly striking. Early natives created circles of incised stones, and dozens still remain in this valley that was sacred to the Diaguita tribes.

Tall standing stones from this region, some 10 feet high, have been collected in Menhir Park. Scholars cannot agree on their age or the meaning of their inscriptions.

Prehistoric ceramics of the Condorhuasi culture are of strange figures with animal and human characteristics.

COLONIAL AND POST-INDEPENDENCE ART After the arrival of the Spanish and throughout colonial times, religious themes dominated artistic expression. Manuel Belgrano founded the School of Geometry, Perspective and Drawing in Buenos Aires during the colonial period.

Two early Argentinean painters of the 1830s were Carlos Morel and Fernando García Molina. Prilidiano Pueyrredón and Cándido López dominated 19th century painting. Benito Quinquela Martín and Uruguayan-born Pedro Figari have depicted life in Buenos Aires in more recent times.

Art movements orginating in Europe, such as impressionism, appealed to many Argentinean painters. Much current work expresses art for its own sake rather than as social commentary. As in other countries, some artists have blurred the distinction between photography, painting, and sculpture. The visual and dramatic arts are sometimes combined in performance pieces.

Among the noteworthy artists who have worked in clay, stone, or ceramics are Lucio Fontana and Fernando Arranz. The sculptures of Julio le Parc and Alicia Peñalba are widely known outside of Argentina. A teaching photographer, Pedro Luis Raota, has won awards in at least 22 countries.

Argentina's artists show their work in more than 100 art galleries in Buenos Aires and additional galleries and museums in the smaller cities.

Opposite, above: **Ethnic Indian handicrafts. Although the Indian civilization did not reach the artistic heights of the Incas in neighboring Peru, it still produced beautiful and highly artistic crafts.**

Opposite, below: **A sculpture in the park. In the bigger cities, sculptures and murals are located in public for everyone to see and appreciate.**

Below: **A wall mural—street art is popular in Argentina.**

GAUCHO ART

Gaucho handicrafts. These handicrafts, the spurs, the knife and the *bolas,* inform us of the kind of life the gaucho leads.

The uniquely Argentinean theme of gaucho life has inspired literature, painting, and music.

Domingo F. Sarmiento, the country's president from 1868 to 1874, attacked the legend of the proud, rebellious gaucho in *Civilization and Barbarism: Life of Juan Facundo Quiroga* (1845). He felt that education, not rebellion, was the key to the country's future. *El Gaucho Martin Fierro* (1872), a famous epic poem by José Hernández, described in vivid detail the difficult life of a gaucho. This masterpiece, called the "national poem," is still read in Argentinian schools. Hernández's portrait was sympathetic to the plight of the gauchos. He portrayed the people they encountered and often fought with—Indians, blacks, the military and the police, and depicted the forces that threatened their way of life.

Novelists influenced by Hernández included Benito Lynch and Ricardo Güiraldes. Güiraldes' *Don Segundo Sombra* (1926) imaginatively portrayed the decline of the gaucho. A group of young writers in the 1920s, known as the *Martinfierristas*, published a literary review called *Martín Fierro*. Jorge Luis Borges, a member of this group, emerged as a nominee for the most important prize in literature, the Noble prize.

The "father of Argentinean national music," Alberto Williams, composed a piece called *Aires de la Pampa* in 1893. One of the best known 20th century composers, Alberto Ginastera, used gaucho dances and songs in many of his compositions.

THE WRITTEN WORD

Many Argentinean writers came to the attention of the outside world when Victoria Ocampo spent a personal fortune to publish their works in the literary magazine *Sur,* which she founded in 1931. She also published short stories and poems of outstanding foreign writers, and her magazine enjoyed international circulation.

Noted 20th century Argentinean writers include Leopoldo Lugones, Manuel Ugarte, Alfredo Palacios, Ernesto Sábato, Julio Cortázar, Manuel Puig, and Adolfo Bioy-Casares.

Italian-born Alfonsina Storni became a leading Argentinean poet. Bioy-Casares collaborated with Jorge Luis Borges and also wrote books of his own, including a chronicle of *porteño* life called *Asleep in the Sun.* Cortázar is known for short stories and novels, such as *Rayuela,* that have been translated into many languages.

Celeste Goes Dancing is an engaging sample in English of stories written in the 1980s by 14 representative Argentinean writers.

Jacobo Timmerman, a newspaper editor, gained international attention with his book *Prisoner Without a Name, Cell Without a Number* (1981). After he had been treated brutally by the military authorities, Timmerman accused them of attacking him not only because he expressed dissent against the government but also because he is a Jew.

A secondhand bookshop. Here one can exchange used books or buy old books at a fraction of their original value.

JORGE LUIS BORGES (1899–1986)

Probably the most famous of Argentinean writers, Jorge Luis Borges' essays, poetry, and short stories inspired an entire generation of writers. He was especially admired for his brilliant use of language and his original thoughts about the meaning of life. Borges' stories convey a sense of mystery and the fantastic. Critics have compared them to the stories of Edgar Allen Poe.

Borges' international outlook may have sprung from his family roots. His father was of Italian, Jewish, and English background, while his mother was Argentinean and Uruguayan. He studied

in Switzerland and published his first poem in Spain. He disapproved of Perón but took no active part in politics. In 1927, Borges began to lose his vision and was completely blind by the age of 56. Through the help of assistants, books and writing remained the central passion of his life. At 68, he wed for the first time, but the marriage was unhappy and did not last. Shortly before his death, he married his 41-year-old secretary and traveling companion.

Among his best-known books available in English are *Ficciónes* (Fictions) and *El Aleph* ("aleph" is the first letter of the Hebrew alphabet). Borges won many literary honors, including Spain's most important literary award in 1980. He was nominated for the Nobel prize for literature several times, but never won it.

Opposite above: **The most famous tango singer was Carlos Gardel. Between 1917, when he invented the tango song, and his death in the 1930s in an airplane crash, Gardel grew into a national hero. His music is as popular today as it was during his lifetime.**

Opposite below: **The tango in motion.**

MUSIC AND DANCE

Composers in Argentina have been influenced by both European models and songs of the gauchos. Jesuit missionaries taught music to the native Indians in the 17th century. Amancio Alcorta (1805–1862) is considered to be the first native-born Argentinean composer. Through the years, many composers, singers, instrumentalists, conductors, dancers, and choreographers from Argentina have achieved international recognition.

Opera, so beloved by Italians, is second only to the tango in popularity. Among the best-known works is Alberto Ginastera's opera *Bomarzo*, remembered for its violence and dramatic impact on audiences. More than 70 Argentinean operas have been produced at home and abroad.

Folk dancing thrives in provinces such as Salta. Many of the best folk dancers are still in their teens. Dance styles echo Inca, Spanish, gaucho, and other Latin-American forms of music and dancing.

ARGENTINA'S TANGO The music everyone identifies with Argentina is the tango ("TAHN-goh"). As a dance, the tango is characterized by a male and female dancer holding each other and gliding together in long steps, occasionally pausing in dramatic poses. The accompanying lyrics are often melancholy musings on lost love.

The tango appeared near the end of the last century and gained worldwide popularity early in the 20th century. Some scholars trace its roots to gypsy music in Spain, while others say it developed from the *milonga* ("mee-LOHN-gah"), an earlier dance popular in Argentina, and from other dances such as the polka. Tango music is generally played by guitar, violin, flute, piano, or especially the *bandoneôn* ("bahn-doh-NYOHN"), a relative of the accordion.

People who dance the tango are called tango interpreters. Originally a form of working-class expression, the tango was at first considered vulgar by the upper classes. In the 1920s, the Pope declared that there was nothing sinful in dancing the tango. Its popularity spread to the upper classes in Buenos Aires and then to other countries around the world. Tango is now performed mostly for tourists.

MUSEUMS AND SCIENTISTS

The National Museum of Fine Arts opened in Buenos Aires in 1896 and soon became a showcase for the works of local artists. Today it houses works of modern Argentinean and foreign artists, as well as 400-year-old paintings illustrating Argentinean history.

Other museums in Buenos Aires include the Museum of Spanish-American Art, with its valuable collection of colonial artifacts and silver, and the Pharmacy Museum, where antiques from apothecaries are on display. The José Hernández Museum specializes in the culture of the gauchos. The city of Rosario has an excellent Museum of Modern Art. La Plata, the Natural Science Museum, founded in 1877, has a world-famous fossil collection. Many fossils housed there came from the pampas and Patagonia, and many of them were discovered by Florentino Ameghino (1854-19ll), one of the world's first paleontologists.

FILM

The movie industry in Argentina developed after World War I. Buenos Aires and Mexico City became the chief producers of films in the Spanish language.

Argentinean movies have won awards in film festivals in many countries. In the United States, *The Official Story* won an Oscar for Best Foreign Film (1985). Actress Norma Aleandro was nominated for Best Actress in that film. She portrayed a woman who discovers that her adopted daughter is the child of one of the "disappeared." A film based on Argentinean Manuel Puig's novel, *Kiss of the Spider Woman,* won the Academy Award for Best Actor (William Hurt) in 1986. This film again depicted governmental persecution of private citizens. In spite of a thriving local film-making industry, movies imported from the United States and Europe are still the most popular in Argentina.

When they are not outdoors playing games, Argentineans love to read, dance, and go to the movies.

Right: **Córdoba University is a beautiful example of colonial architecture. Built in 1613, it was the first university in Argentina.**

Below: **The Teatro Colón is one of the world's largest and most elegant opera houses. Built between 1887 and 1908, it is considered the finest concert hall in Latin America.**

ARCHITECTURE

Colonial architectural styles are especially well-preserved in northern Argentina. A handsome example is Córdoba's cathedral, completed in 1784. Like the cities in Spain, most towns in Argentina are built around a main square. The cathedral and chief government buildings face this plaza. In the countryside, many lavish estates were also built in the Spanish style.

Buenos Aires shows the influence of Spanish and Italian architecture, but many visitors feel it resembles Paris most of all. Wide boulevards, apartment buildings with balconies, and large government buildings dating from the 19th century remind many visitors of the French capital. Numerous gardens, many containing marble statues, add to the beauty of the city.

BENITO QUINQUELA MARTÍN AND LA BOCA

If one artist could change the look of a city, painter Benito Quinquela Martín was the person to do it. He built a primary school for the children of La Boca, formely a slum area of Buenos Aires. When he gave the school to the city, it was on condition that it also house a museum of waterfront paintings. As a result, La Boca became an art colony, with Quinquela Martín as one of its most talented painters.

He also persuaded a number of restaurant owners in La Boca to paint their buildings in bright colors. Owners of run-down homes in the neighborhood followed suit, painting them in vivid reds, yellows, and blues. He also established an open-air market to promote local artists.

This river-front section in the city remains a favorite gathering spot for painters, sculptors, and poets. Tourists enjoy the colorful buildings and restaurants. Spirited music in the clubs reminds them that the tango first appeared in the dance-halls of La Boca.

LEISURE

ARGENTINEANS enjoy a climate that favors outdoor activities throughout the year. The name Buenos Aires comes from the early Spaniards' gratitude to the Virgin of the Good Winds for their safe arrival in this delightful land. Today, Argentineans are still grateful for good winds and fresh air near their beautiful lakes and rivers, the Atlantic Ocean, and the majestic Andes mountains. They camp, hunt, fish, hike, climb rock faces and mountains, ski, sail, windsurf, cycle, and play tennis, squash, and golf. They take seaside vacations on the Atlantic coast and inland vacations in resort areas such as Bariloche.

Besides these individual and family pursuits, Argentineans love team sports. They like to play them and to watch them, cheering for their favorite teams and players. You'll find them watching everything from basketball and cricket to rugby and football, all games with an international appeal.

They also like rugged contests on horseback, some of which are unique to Argentina. Unlike many other Spanish-speaking countries, however, Argentina does not practice the cruel sport of bullfighting.

Opposite: **Clowns in the park. Argentina is blessed with a cool and refreshing climate that favors outdoor activities.**

Below: **Children at Iguazú Falls. The rock pools around the falls are good bathing and wading areas.**

A PASSION FOR SOCCER

Probably the most popular sport in Argentina is soccer, known as *fútbol*. The English brought this game to Argentina in the 19th century.

Children grow up playing soccer at school, in the street, or in any open space. Competition to be selected for a boys' team is fierce, and those boys

The dream of almost every Argentinean boy is to be rich and famous by becoming a soccer superstar.

who grow up to become professional soccer players earn top salaries. They often become national heroes.

In Buenos Aires, a traditional rivalry pits the Boca Juniors, from the Italian neighborhood of La Boca, against the River Plate team. Three-quarters of the nation's fans support one of those two teams.

Among national teams, a passionate rivalry exists between Argentina and Brazil. In the past, more than 100,000 fans have turned out to watch individual games between the two countries.

Some of the country's best soccer players leave to play for the wealthier club teams of other countries, especially in Spain and Italy. Brazil and Mexico also hire Argentinean players. However, these soccer stars often return home to compete for Argentina in the World Cup championship games.

Argentina's soccer honors include the Junior World Championship in 1979 and the World Cup in 1978 and 1986, when they defeated Holland in their first triumph and West Germany in their second. In the 1990 tournament, after defeating both archrivals Brazil and home-favorites Italy, they lost to West Germany in the final. Sergio Goycoechea, the substitute goalkeeper who stepped in as replacement in the final matches, became a national hero with his superb and inspirational play.

Argentina's Maradona and his teammates celebrate their winning goal against Brazil in a 1990 World Cup match.

SMALL BUT MIGHTY

A few years ago, Argentina's Diego Maradona was considered the best soccer player in the world. His fiery personality, tremendous athletic skill, and superb performances have made him the subject of many stories. The 5-foot-5-inch star from the Villa Fiorito slum in Buenos Aires has been called everything from Argentina's "Golden Boy" and "king of soccer" to "explosive," "spoiled," and "Mr. Disagreeable." He wears No. 10 on his jersey, traditionally given to a team's best scorer; it is also the number of soccer's greatest star, Pele. Like Pele, his life is a rags to riches story.

Until 1991, Maradona played as an attacking midfielder for the Italian team, Napoli. He was a serious factor in their winning the highly competitive Italian championship, but has since left them after a cocaine abuse conviction. He now plays for the Argentinean team Newell's Old Boys. Because of his drug conviction, he was banned from playing soccer for 18 months. However, he has regained his fitness and is expected to captain for Argentina in the 1994 World Cup soccer finals in the United States. His presence and reputation will be an inspiration for the team.

In polo, players on ponies try to hit a wooden ball into goals at either end of a 295-yard-long playing field. Four players are on a team, and the game has five or six periods, called *chukkers*.

BRITISH HORSEBACK

The gaucho tradition of great horsemanship still influences Argentinean sports. The game of polo, played on specially-bred ponies, was brought by the British and flourished in Argentina.

In Buenos Aires, crowds of 20,000 routinely turn out to cheer for their favorite players, such as Gonzalo Pieres, a national hero who is ranked as one of the world's best.

Players begin their training as children, swinging little mallets from bicycles. Then they play in leagues similar to those for soccer. The best polo players own farms where they can practice year-round. Family teams of fathers, sons, uncles, and cousins are common.

Prized for their speed and ability to work with their riders, Argentinean polo ponies may cost up to $6,000 apiece.

Show-jumping is another sport in which local riders and horses have gained international attention. Both the National Polo Fields and the famous Argentine Horsetrack are in Palermo, a northern suburb of Buenos Aires. Argentineans love to go to horse races. To cater to this, a newer turf race track has been built in the Buenos Aires suburb of San Isidro.

GAUCHO HORSEBACK

A game on horseback called *pato* ("PAH-toh") originated from the gauchos. *Pato* was originally played using a live duck (*pato* in Spanish). The duck was placed in a sack with its head sticking out. Two teams would race over a three-mile-long field fighting over the sack. The frequently bloody fights that ensued led to the game being banned in 1822. But it resurfaced under President Juan Manuel de Rosas. Today, a six-handled, inflated leather bag replaces the duck.

To score points, players must land the bag in a netted iron hoop three feet in diameter at the opponent's end of the playing field. *Pato* has mostly been a working-class game, but its popularity is spreading among other social groups. As in the more upper-class game of polo, *pato* horses are valued for their speed, strength, endurance, and ability to work with their riders.

In the game of *sortija* ("sor-TEE-ha"), a horseman gallops at full speed and tries to lance a small ring hanging from a bar. Much skill is needed, as the ring may be as tiny as a wedding ring.

Rodeos are popular in many parts of Argentina, with roping and riding contests where descendants of the gauchos demonstrate their traditional skills. The most important rodeo is held each May at Ayacucho.

99

- Opposite: **Juan Fangio.**

RACING LEGEND JUAN FANGIO

Like soccer star Diego Maradona, Juan Manuel Fangio (b. 1911) was born in poverty but acquired international fame and wealth through competitive sports.

In the 1950s, when Fangio won the Grand Prix championship five times ('51, '54, '55, '56, '59), the lives of racing drivers were both glamorous and risky. Drivers wore neither hard helmets nor flame-proof clothing. Thirty drivers—all Fangio's friends—died in flaming wrecks during that decade. Because cars today have better brakes, wider tires, and more safety features, there are far fewer fatal accidents.

In his autobiography, Fangio devotes an entire chapter to the topic of luck. He believes that "no one dies before the day that is marked." He has been accused of being cold-blooded, and in fact, old newsreels show him driving skillfully past burning wrecks that roll into screaming spectators. "When someone was killed, I thought to myself, surely he committed an error," he has said. Fangio trusted his skills, his mechanics, and his cars. He had two accidents in which his co-driver died. He blamed those crashes on his lack of sleep.

Fangio grew up poor and worked long hours from childhood in a garage. Perhaps it was there that he gained the mystical ability his competitors said allowed him to communicate with the steel, engines, and tires of his cars. His first race was in a 1929 Ford taxi, but he later won races driving Alfa Romeos, Mercedes, Ferraris, and Maseratis. He retired while still on top and became president of Mercedes-Benz in South America. In 1990, at 79, he was still honorary company president for life, going to the office each day in spite of having undergone five heart surgery operations. Fangio founded an auto museum in his hometown of Balcarce, where 500 of his trophies and 50 of his racing and classic cars are on display.

SCALING THE HEIGHTS

In early August, a snow carnival and the annual national ski championships are held in Bariloche.

Mountain climbers from many countries come to Argentina to attempt to scale the Andes peaks. Mendoza, about 800 miles west of Buenos Aires, is the chief province for mountain climbing.

Mt. Aconcagua, the highest peak in the Western Hemisphere, provides the ultimate challenge. It was first climbed by Matias Zurbriggen of Switzerland in 1897.

There are 10 recognized routes up this mountain, but most climbers use the northern route.

Teams from West Germany, Italy, Switzerland, and the United States have climbed here. The mountain has claimed many lives; climbers that died on the mountain are buried in a small cemetery at the foot of the mountain.

For people who prefer to go up and down with the help of wings, another adventurous sport, hang-gliding, is rather popular. It is sponsored by the Air Force. International competitions are held in the hills near Córdoba, an area famous for challenging wind drafts.

COMPETITIVE SPORTS CREATE HEROES

As the section on Juan Fangio reveals, professional auto racing is a much-loved sport in Argentina. While Fangio was a world champion driver five times, other Argentineans, like Carlos Alberto Reutemann, a famous Grand Prix driver, and Ricardo Zunino, who already has a top reputation in this field, have taken over his mantle.

Of the well-known Argentinean boxers, the most famous is probably Luis Angel Firpo, who fought in the 1920s. He was called "The Wild Bull of the Pampas" and is honored with a statue in Buenos Aires. He once knocked world heavyweight champion Jack Dempsey out of the ring in 1923, but lost that match. Other Argentinean boxers have been world champions in various weight classes, including Carlos Monzón, who held the middleweight title from 1970 to 1977.

Among the many titles and trophies won by Argentinean athletes is the world championship ice hockey title in 1978, many swimming records, plus golf and marathon-running awards. Argentina's international tennis stars include Guillermo Vilas, José Luis Clerc, Ivanna Madruga, and Gabriela Sabatini. Rugby star Hugo Porta is considered one of the greatest players of all time.

Fishing becomes competitive when national and international championships are held in Bariloche each year. A record 36-pound trout was caught in that region. Competitions are also held each year in Paso de la Patria, a town on the Paraná River in the northeast. People try and catch the largest golden Dorado, a fighting fish that can weigh up to 60 pounds.

Argentina has produced several chess world champions. Youthful stars have included world champion Oscar Panno in 1952, Carlos Bielicki in 1957, and world cadet champion Marcelo Tempone in 1979.

By the time he had retired from racing in 1959, Juan Fangio had won 16 world championship Grand Prix races, including four consecutive German title races.

FESTIVALS

ARGENTINA is alive with festivals, or *fiestas* ("fee-EHS-tahs"). Their colorful processions brighten the landscape from one end of the country to the other. Many different groups of people express their artistic, musical, and culinary creativity through festival celebrations. Argentinean festivals reflect the spiritual traditions of both native Indian religions and Christianity.

Some historical events are remembered through festivals. For example, each provincial city celebrates the anniversary of its founding. In other festivals, the people celebrate legends and myths of the many cultures that have enriched Argentina.

Festivals and holidays may involve religious pilgrimages, feasts, parades, dancing, and even gaucho competitions on horseback. Most of the competitors in these last events are descendants of gauchos. They use traditional old costumes and saddles for the contest. A noted example, the Gaucho Festival of San Antonio de Areco, 80 miles north of Buenos Aires, takes place from November 10 to 17.

The traditions of immigrant communities form the basis for some festivals. A noted one, the Welsh singing festival, takes place in October in Trevelin, a Patagonian mountain town near Esquel. A gathering of Welsh poets and musicians also takes place each year at Gaiman in Patagonia.

Opposite: **Santa Claus in Buenos Aires. Christmas is widely and joyously celebrated in this Catholic land.**

Below: **No parade would be complete without the smart and crisp displays of marching soldiers.**

WINE, MATE, WHEAT, AND PONCHOS

Some festivals celebrate the chief products of a region. In Mendoza, the wine-growing area along the Andes, the Vendimia Festival is celebrated in March, to mark the grape harvest. It honors more than 1,500 wine producers from that part of Argentina. It is one of the most impressive festivals in Latin America. The vines are blessed, fountains of free red wine are available to the thirsty crowd, a festival queen reigns, and an impressive parade is held. The people of Mendoza also celebrate their history. Toward the end of February, before the wine festival, it commemorates General San Martín's crossing of the Andes.

May 25, one of Argentina's two Independence Days. People dress in costumes and masks of the early 19th century to reenact the declaration of independence.

In Posadas, the capital of the province of Misiones, there is an annual festival to celebrate the harvest of the *mate* ("MAH-teh") crop. *Mate* is a kind of holly brewed to make a tea that is so popular it's considered the national drink. Ornately decorated coaches carrying the prettiest girls from each district of the province parade through the streets. One of the girls is chosen to serve as the year's *Mate* Queen.

The most important wheat festival in Argentina takes place in Leones, in the province of Córdoba. A wheat queen reigns over the commercial and industrial fair with its related folklore events. People in the central farming provinces celebrate many harvest festivals.

The Fiesta del Poncho in Catamarca features the local production of hand–woven ponchos. The fleece for these objects comes from three animals that can live at high altitudes: the alpaca, the llama, and the vicuña. The people who proudly display their ponchos are continuing an ancient tradition. For the gauchos, ponchos were an indispensable piece of clothing. Today, tourists prize them for their artistry as well as their usefulness.

CARNIVAL

Carnival occurs at the same time as similar celebrations among Roman Catholics all over the world, including the Mardi Gras in the United States. The celebration of Carnival in Argentina is especially vigorous in the northern part of the country. Business comes to a halt as costumed Argentineans dance in the streets.

Carnival festivities usually begin on the weekend before Ash Wednesday, which most often falls in February. The celebrations are mixed with Indian traditions in the northeast. In Tilcara, floral arrangements representing the Stations of the Cross are hung along the streets. Processions come down from the mountains on Ash Wednesday.

In many parts, Carnival is not celebrated with the same abandon as in Brazil. But visitors may find that the majority of people will party and that business and social life are far from normal during Carnival. Celebrants may be expected to finish a large cup of some alcoholic drink in a single gulp. They also may be doused by water-filled balloons. They will encounter balls and parties in the hotels and clubs of major cities.

The yearly Carnival traditionally represents the people's last opportunity to make merry before earnest fasting and praying begins during the season of Lent.

The Tango Festival begins in the first half of January and kicks off a series of fiestas all across the country.

REGIONAL FESTIVALS

Every month of the calendar has its share of colorful regional festivals. In Puerto Madryn, an underwater fishing festival kicks off the New Year. In Rosario del Tala, a Tango Festival runs through the first half of January. The last half of January is devoted to a two-week National Folklore Festival in Cosquín in the province of Córdoba. An artisan fair held at the same time adds to the festivities.

On February 2, processions on horseback at Humahuaca near Jujuy bring pilgrims to the Candelaria Virgin. Fireworks, traditional foods, and religious music add to the celebration. Northern Argentineans meet with southern Bolivians during the Easter week to trade handicrafts and other goods and again on the last two Sundays in October at the *Manca Fiesta* (Festival of the Pot), where merchandise is traded once more.

Salta Week, June 14–20, marks the anniversary of a local battle. While San Martín was fighting the Spanish, Salta's town hero, General Martín

Miguel de Güemes, led a band of gauchos against the Spanish in the Gaucho War. This festival includes fireworks displays, colorful floats, singing, and dancing. Salta is also noted for its Christmas performances, tableaus, and carol singing, which go on for weeks.

Corrientes, which has a particularly lively Carnival celebration, marks its founding on May 3 with a religious and popular arts festival.

On June 24, St. John's Day is celebrated in several towns, most unusually in Formosa, where the faithful walk barefoot over a bed of hot coals. Processions in Salta, Jujuy, and Mendoza honor St. James each year on July 25. St. Ann is honored a day later in Tilcara, near Jujuy.

Argentineans also enjoy gathering for the annual Livestock Exhibition in July at the Argentine Rural Society in Buenos Aires. Cattle, horses, sheep, and pigs are judged for prizes and sold at auction.

Historical events are celebrated throughout the country with much pomp and ceremony.

The small village of Villa General Belgrano hosts an Alpine Chocolate Festival each winter and an authentic Oktoberfest (beer festival).

Several times during the year, thousands of Catholics make a pilgrimage to celebrate the Fiesta of our Lady of Luján, the patron saint of Argentina. Many walk from their homes all the way to Luján. Early in December, old coaches from a provincial colonial museum in Luján are paraded around the town, with the people dressed in colonial costume.

MUSICAL CELEBRATIONS

The northwest of Argentina is famed for its beautiful colonial architecture, being one of the areas where the Spanish first settled. But at the same time, it remains the heart of Indian culture. The regions history has contributed to the unique, present-day musical celebrations that fuse both Indian and Spanish traditions.

Folk music is very much alive in Argentina.

The traditional customs of the Indians are still preserved in colorful celebrations like the *misachicos* ("mee-sah-CHEE-kos"), the carnival of Jujy, and some other religious festivals.

During these occasions, musicians will come down from the hills to crowd the narrow, steep streets of the white villages. They bring with them their *erkes* ("EHR-kes"—long trumpets with a distinctive sound that can easily be heard from a long distance), *charangos* ("chah-RAHN-gos"—instruments made out of the carcasses of a local armadillo called the *mulita*), and typical bass drums.

The music of the people who lived here long before the Spanish arrived survives in these celebrations with their merry and happy songs and dances. *Carnavalitos, bagualas, zambas, cuecas,* and *chacareras* are some local musical expressions, played with typical indigenous instruments like *erkes, charangos,* bass drums, *bombos, sikus,* and *quenas,* mixed with some other European instruments such as guitars, violins, and large accordions.

TWO INDEPENDENCE DAYS

The long standing rivalry between the people of Buenos Aires and the people of the provinces has resulted in Argentineans celebrating two national independence days.

May 25 marks the date when the people of Buenos Aires threw off the Spanish yoke. The people of the interior are honored by the holiday on July 9, when deputies of the interior Congress of Tucumán declared the United Provinces free. Now people in the capital and in the countryside celebrate both holidays.

During the May 25 celebrations a lavish and excitng parade is held. The city plaza is full with army officers in riding boots, naval officers in 19th century frock coats and spats, and soldiers massed in battle gear and black berets in a reenactment of the struggle towards nationhood. As the proud symbol of Argentina, the regal gauchos ride on horseback, their red cloaks flowing in the wind.

PUBLIC HOLIDAYS

Official public holidays include both religious and historical commemorations.

January 1	New Year's Day
January 6	Epiphany
March/April	Good Friday, Easter Sunday, and Maundy Thursday
May 1	Labor Day
May 25	Anniversary of Revolution of 1810
June 10	Malvinas Day—commemorating the Falklands War
June 20	Flag Day
July 9	Independence Day
August 17	Anniversary of the death of General Jose de San Martín, the liberator of Argentina
October 12	Columbus Day
December 8	Catholic feast of the Immaculate Conception
December 25	Christmas

FOOD

In Argentina, the saying goes, everyone is an expert at barbecuing, and no wonder. Beef is by far the most popular food, and some people eat it three times a day.

Traditionally, meat was spit-roasted in the courtyard of the home or in the fields. It was often impaled on a cross-shaped spit, one end of which was driven into the ground at an angle to keep the roast over the flames. At other times, it was cooked on a grill over hot coals.

Today, the average Argentinean consumes 190 pounds of beef every year. Writers have attributed the overwhelming popularity of beef to a belief that eating it gives people the animal's vitality, and that people must eat plenty of it to be strong. Perhaps the real reason so much beef is eaten is that it is plentiful and cheap. Many people consider Argentinean beef the best in the world, tender enough to be cut with a fork.

The typical meal today is grilled beef with French-fried potatoes, salad, and red wine. In restaurants, beef is served in hearty portions. Some restaurants place a small stove at each table and barbecue the meats in front of hungry customers. The meat is salted before it reaches the table.

It is not unusual for workers to choose one of their number to go to the butcher. He or she buys fresh meat, then they roast or grill the meat and share it for lunch.

Argentineans are slowly absorbing the news that eating less meat may lower cholesterol levels and improve health. But they enter the 90s with beef still their favorite food.

Opposite: **An ice-cream seller doing his acrobatic act for the camera.**

Below: **Beef is so popular in Argentina that people often barbecue a whole cow over an open fire.**

Argentineans are great
meat eaters.

ARGENTINEAN MEALS

Aside from the predictable main course, side dishes can have an Argentinean flair. *Matambre* ("mah-TAHM-breh"), meaning "hunger killer," is an appetizer of marinated flank steak stuffed with spinach, hearts of palm, ham, or hard-boiled eggs and then baked. It is eaten hot or cold.

Lettuce and tomato salads are dressed with oil—often olive oil—and vinegar or lemon juice. The creamy and cheesy salad dressings of the United States are rarely used.

Desserts include fresh fruit and cheese and the much-loved *dulce de leche* ("DOOL-seh de LEH-cheh")—milk simmered with sugar until very thick. This sweet concoction serves as a base for other desserts.

Alfajores con dulce de leche is a confection with two layers of dough surrounding a filling, with a coating over all. Each region of the country has its own style. Happily for chocolate lovers, the chocolate versions are plentiful and delicious. *Dulce de leche* is also spread on breakfast toast, eaten by the spoonful, served along with ice cream, and used in cakes and meringues. Sometimes it is eaten with cheese to cut the sweetness.

Rice pudding and *almendrado* ("ahl-mehn-DRAH-doh"), ice cream rolled in crushed almonds, also satisfy the Argentinean sweet tooth. Italian-style ice creams abound in all parts of Argentina.

114

NATIVE FOOD

One of the few truly native dishes to be found in Argentina is *locro* ("LAW-kroh"), a soup or thick corn (maize) stew. *Locro* contains beef, beans, potatoes, peppers, onions, and many other ingredients.

Sweets and candies of all shapes and colors can be found at street-side stalls.

The Indian influence on food is most noticeable in the north. In the northeast, near the famous Iguazú Falls, typical Guaraní dishes include *chipa* ("CHEE-pah"), a small, hard biscuit made of manioc (a starchy vegetable), eggs, and cheese.

Sopa Paraguaya ("SOH-pah pah-rah-WAH-zhah") is a pie made of corn, cheese, and eggs. *Reviro* ("reh-VEE-roh") is made of dried meat, onions, and spices fried together.

In the northwest, too, certain dishes reflect the *mestizo* heritage. *Humita en chala* is a mildly spicy cornmeal tamale cooked in corn husks.

Above: **A typical meal consists of grilled beef, salad, french fries, and red wine.**

Opposite top: **A man cooking** *empanadas.* **Such snacks are handy for tea or if there is no time to eat in a restaurant.**

Opposite bottom: **The Italian connection. Pizza has been adopted as part of the local diet in the cities due to the large inflow of Italian immigrants.**

INTERNATIONAL INFLUENCE

The food of Argentina is really a blend of Italian, Jewish, Spanish, Polish, German, and Chinese foods. Only the Indian dishes can be considered truly native. The rest of Argentinean cuisine arrived with immigrants and reflects the many different ethnic groups in the country.

The gauchos contributed the *asado,* beef roasted over an open wood or coal fire. Argentinean variations on beef include: *bife a caballo* ("BEE-feh ah kah-VAH-zhoh"—beef on horseback)—steak topped with fried eggs; *carbonada* ("kar-bao-NAH-dah")—stew of beef, corn, squash, and peaches baked in a pumpkin shell; *churrasco* ("choor-RAHS-koh")—grilled steak; *chorizos* ("choh-REE-sohs")—spicy sausages; and *morcillas* (mohr-SEE-zhas")—blood sausage from German and Polish cooking.

At the *parrillada* ("par-ree-ZHAH-da"), a grill house that cooks meats over charcoal fires, one can order a *parrillada mixta,* or mixed grill. Some Argentineans enjoy grilling an assortment of sausages, short ribs, and organ meats such as kidneys, liver, and sweetbreads, and even the cow's intestines and udder.

From Europe comes *milanesa,* thinly-sliced beef covered with beaten egg and bread crumbs and then deep-fried. Besides beef, Argentineans eat roasted or grilled pork, goat and lamb. Spanish cooking inspired *puchero de gallina,* a chicken stew made with corn, sausages, potatoes, and squash. Children especially like *ñoquis,* which are potato dumplings served with meat and tomato sauce. Argentinean *empanadas* are derived from Britain's Cornish pasties. They are fried or baked pastries in a crescent shape, stuffed with chopped meats, cheese, creamed corn, other vegetables, fish or seafood. Chopped hardboiled egg, olives, raisins and onions sometimes flavor the filling

FINDING FOOD

Eating out is a favorite activity in Argentina. There are many types of restaurants and shops that cater to hungry diners. The great majority of restaurants feature beef. Some seat hundreds of people and are busy at all hours. People linger for hours over a three-course meal, with orchestras entertaining them.

Sidewalk cafes line the wide boulevards of Buenos Aires. Argentineans take advantage of a moderate climate by lingering at outdoor tables as they take an English-style afternoon tea break.

The names of food shops sound like pure poetry ... *pizzerías*, *cafeterías*, *heladerías* for ice cream, and *confiterías* for cakes, sandwiches, *empanadas*, and simple main dishes. *Confiterías* stay open from the early morning to midnight. Because most restaurants offer the same menu at both lunch and dinner, the *confiteria* is the place to go for a light noon-day meal.   *Porteños* tend to eat a light breakfast, a large lunch between noon and 3 p.m., late-afternoon tea and pastry, and a huge late dinner between 10 p.m. and midnight. Restaurants usually stay open until 2 a.m.

RECIPE: BIFE A CABALLO ("BEEF ON HORSEBACK")

Ingredients:	one beef steak (per person)	olive oil
	one egg (per person)	pinch of salt

Method: Coat the steak with olive oil and sprinkle with salt. Grill steak to desired redness, preferably on a charcoal grill or barbeque. Separately, fry egg sunny side up. When steak is cooked, place egg on top of steak. Serve with mixed salad and crusty bread.

WINE AND OTHER SPIRITS

The wines of Argentina are considered some of the best in South America. Argentina produces its own beer, whiskey, rum, vodka, and other liquors, but it exports only its wines. The wines of Mendoza are well-loved throughout the country. Most Argentineans drink red wine with their meals. A highly-prized type is called Malbec. White wines are produced in the Salta region and are exported even to Germany.

Chilean wine is also served in many restaurants in Argentina. Wine and champagne coolers with fruit mixed in by the bartender are popular summer drinks. A slightly alcoholic cider, called *sidra,* is featured at the famous Café Tortoni. *Whiskerías* are numerous in Buenos Aires. These informal cocktail lounges also serve sandwiches. In general, the people of Argentina tend to chat over coffee or a soft drink rather than over cocktails. While they love to drink wine with meals, Argentineans also enjoy their food with carbonated mineral water.

Inside a rural *whiskería,* a bartender chats with his lone customer.

119

Maté cups and containers come in various shapes and sizes.

YERBA MATE

Maté (pronounced mah'-tay) is a type of tea made from the young leaves of an evergreen tree of the holly family known as Brazilian holly. The tea leaves come both from trees grown on plantations and from trees growing wild in the Misiones jungles. Also known as "Paraguayan tea," this drink is commonly called *yerba maté*.

To prepare it, the greenish herb is ground to the size of ordinary tea leaves. The leaves are steeped in very hot water in a gourd or bowl and then drunk from a small hole in the top through a metal straw called a *bombilla*. The straw has a filter to keep the leaves out of one's mouth. The bowl and the *bombilla* may be ornately decorated, often with silver. *Yerba maté* was developed by the native Indians, adopted by the gauchos, and finally taken over by the entire country.

In home parties, *maté* may be served plain or with sugar, anise seeds, orange peel or milk. The drink is sometimes shared socially, passing from person to person. Like regular tea, it contains some caffeine. The gauchos found it pepped them up and helped them to go for long stretches without food or sleep.

A *yerba maté* plantation.

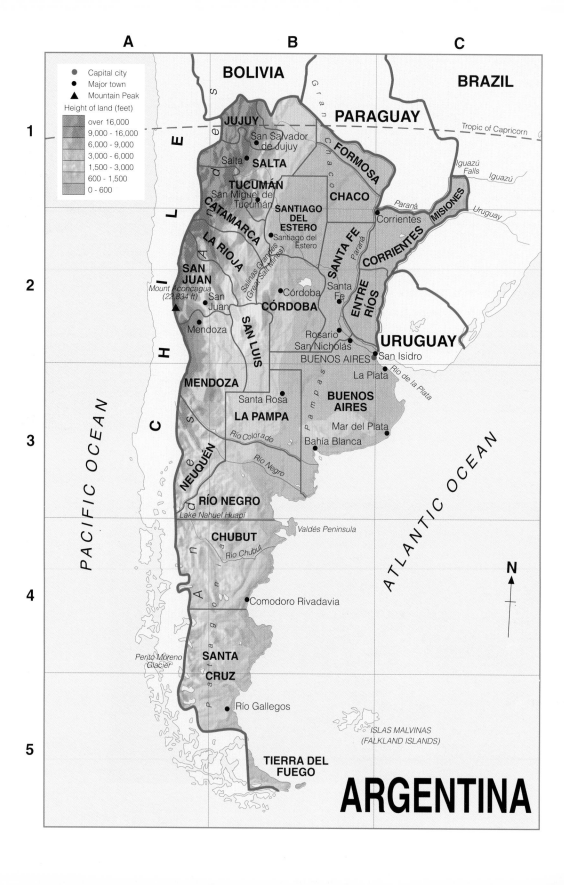

A　　　　　　**B**　　　　　　**C**

BOLIVIA

BRAZIL

PARAGUAY

Tropic of Capricorn

1

JUJUY

San Salvador
de Jujuy ●

Salta ● **SALTA**

FORMOSA

Iguazú
Falls

Iguazú

TUCUMÁN

San Miguel de
Tucumán

CHACO

CATAMARCA

**SANTIAGO
DEL
ESTERO**

Paraná

Corrientes ●

MISIONES

Uruguay

LA RIOJA

Santiago del
Estero ●

SANTA FE

CORRIENTES

Paraná

**SAN
JUAN**

Salinas Grandes
(Great Salt Mines)

2

Mount Aconcagua
(22,834 ft)
▲ San
Juan ●

● Córdoba

Santa
Fe ●

**ENTRE
RÍOS**

CÓRDOBA

● Mendoza

Rosario ●

URUGUAY

SAN LUIS

San Nicholás ●

BUENOS AIRES

San Isidro ●

La Plata ●

Río de la Plata

MENDOZA

Santa Rosa ●

**BUENOS
AIRES**

LA PAMPA

Mar del Plata ●

3

Río Colorado

Bahía Blanca ●

Río Negro

NEUQUÉN

RÍO NEGRO

Lake Nahuel Huapí

Valdés Peninsula

CHUBUT

Río Chubut

4

Comodoro Rivadavia ●

N

Perito Moreno
Glacier

**SANTA
CRUZ**

● Río Gallegos

ISLAS MALVINAS
(FALKLAND ISLANDS)

5

**TIERRA DEL
FUEGO**

ARGENTINA

PACIFIC OCEAN

ATLANTIC OCEAN

● Capital city
● Major town
▲ Mountain Peak

Height of land (feet)
over 16,000
9,000 - 16,000
6,000 - 9,000
3,000 - 6,000
1,500 - 3,000
600 - 1,500
0 - 600

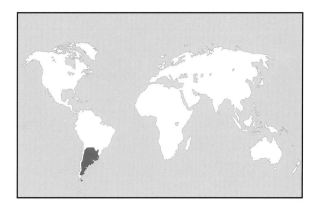

QUICK NOTES

LAND AREA
1,073,400 square miles
(400,000 square miles of additional
territory in dispute)

POPULATION
33.5 million

CAPITAL
Buenos Aires

PROVINCES
Buenos Aires, Catamarca, Chaco, Chubut,
Córdoba, Corrientes, Distrito Federal, Entre
Ríos, Formosa, Jujuy, La Pampa, La Rioja,
Mendoza, Misiones, Neuquén, Río Negro,
Salta, San Juan, San Luis, Santa Cruz, Santa
Fé, Santiago del Estero, Tierra del Fuego
and part of Antarctica and South Atlantic
Islands (national territory), Tucumán.

NATIONAL LANGUAGE
Spanish

MAJOR RELIGION
Roman Catholicism

CURRENCY
Austral, divided into 100 centavos
Value against $US changes periodically

MAIN EXPORTS
Meat, wheat, corn, oilseed, hides, wool,
fruits, nuts

IMPORTANT ANNIVERSARIES
Labor Day, Constitution of 1853 (May 1)
National Day, Anniversary of the 1810
    Revolution (May 25)
Malvinas Day, commemorating Falkland
    Islands War of 1982 (June 10)
Flag Day (June 20)
Independence from Spain in 1816 (July 9)
Death of General José de San Martín
    (August 17)
Columbus Day (October 12)

POLITICAL LEADERS
General José de San Martín (1778–1850)—
    liberator.
General Manuel Belgrano (1770–1820)—
    revolutionary who created the national
    flag.
Bernardino Rivadavia (1780–1845)—first
    president of Argentina (1826–1827).
Domingo Faustino Sarmiento (1811–
    1888)—president (1868–1874) who
    contributed greatly to public education.
General Juan Perón (1895–1974)—
    influential former president (1946–1955
    and 1973–1974).
Carlos Saúl Menem—president (1989–).

GLOSSARY

bola ("BOH-lah") A long rope ending in two or three pieces tied to hard balls covered with leather. It is used for hunting by gauchos; it is thrown in a way that entangles the legs of a running animal.

criollo ("kree-OH-yoh") A person born in Latin America, but of European descent.

estancia ("ess-TAHN-see-ah") A large cattle ranch.

gaucho ("GAH-oo-choh") A horseman and cowboy of the pampas, usually a *mestizo.*

lunfardo ("loon-FAR-doh") A slang language, originally used by the criminals of Buenos Aires. It is used in tango music, popular songs, poetry, and the theater.

mestizo ("mess-TEE-soh") A person of mixed European and Indian ancestry.

pampas ("PAHM-pahs") The flat grass plains of central Argentina.

pato ("PAH-toh") A sport played on horseback, in which players attempt to throw a six-handled leather ball into a net at the opposing team's end of the playing field.

porteños ("porr-TEH-nyos") The people of the city of Buenos Aires.

tango ("TAHN-goh") A dance, accompanied by music, in which a couple hold each other and take long, gliding steps together, occasionally pausing in a dramatic pose.

yerba mate ("ZHER-bah MAH-teh") A holly tea sipped from a gourd through a metal straw.

BIBLIOGRAPHY

Argentina in Pictures, Lerner Publications Company, Minneapolis, 1988.

Fox, Geoffrey E., *The Land and People of Argentina*, Lippencott, New York, 1990.

Hernández, José, *The Gaúcho Martin Fierro*, Editorial Pampa, Buenos Aires, 1960. Adapted from the Spanish and rendered into English verse by Walter Owen with drawings by Alberto Guiraldez.

Hintz, Martin, *Argentina*, Chicago Children's Press, Chicago, 1985.

Huber, Alex, *We Live in Argentina*, The Bookwright Press, New York, 1984.

INDEX

INDEX

INDEX

PICTURE CREDITS:

Victor Englebert
Eduardo Gil
Hulton Deutsch
John Maier, Jr.
Marion Morrison
Tony Morrison
The Hutchison Library
The Image Bank
Tony Perrottet